CW00023079

"*The Interpersonal Solution to Depression* by Pettit and Joiner is an outstanding source of information and advice for those suffering depression, for concerned family members, and for therapists looking for an adjunct to treatment. The authors provide concrete suggestions that are practical, engaging, and based on the best empirical evidence. Experienced therapists, therapy researchers, and graduate students who are interested in combining interpersonal interventions with other approaches to the treatment of depression will find a wealth of insights and suggestions. This is a great book and the innovative, practical guidelines will be universally helpful. It is a self-help book that can either stand alone or play a supportive role in the context of therapy."

> —*Steven R. H. Beach, Ph.D., author of* Depression in Marriage: A Model for Etiology and Treatment *as well as over 100 empirical publications on marriage and marital therapy*

The
Interpersonal
Solution to Depression

A Workbook for Changing How You Feel by Changing How You Relate

JEREMY W. PETTIT, PH.D.

THOMAS ELLIS JOINER, JR., PH.D.

New Harbinger Publications, Inc.

Publisher's Note

This publication is designed to provide accurate and authoritative information in regard to the subject matter covered. It is sold with the understanding that the publisher is not engaged in rendering psychological, financial, legal, or other professional services. If expert assistance or counseling is needed, the services of a competent professional should be sought.

Distributed in Canada by Raincoast Books

Copyright © 2005 by Jeremy Pettit and Thomas Ellis Joiner
New Harbinger Publications, Inc.
5674 Shattuck Avenue
Oakland, CA 94609

Cover design by Amy Shoup
Cover image: Ryan McVay/Getty Images
Acquired by Catharine Sutker
Edited by Jessica Beebe
Text design by Tracy Marie Carlson

ISBN 1-57224-418-6 Paperback

All Rights Reserved

Printed in the United States of America

Library of Congress Cataloging-in-Publication Data

Pettit, Jeremy W.
    The interpersonal solution to depression : a workbook for changing how you feel by changing how you relate / Jeremy W. Pettit and Thomas Ellis Joiner.
        p. cm.
    Includes bibliographical references.
    ISBN 1-57224-418-6
    1. Depression, Mental—Social aspects. 2. Depression, Mental—Treatment—Popular works. 3. Depression, Mental—Treatment—Problems, exercises, etc. 4. Interpersonal psychotherapy. I. Joiner, Thomas E. II. Title.
    RC537.P439 2005
    616.85'2706—dc22
                                        2005018918

New Harbinger Publications' Web site address: www.newharbinger.com

07   06   05

10   9   8   7   6   5   4   3   2   1

First printing

For my parents.

—JWP

Contents

Foreword

The book is innovative in its interpersonal view of depression. Most psychological theories of depression view depression as residing inside the individual in distorted thoughts or beliefs or in skill deficits. This book views depression through a very different lens. Depression is seen as having its basis in our interactions with people in our world. Problems in human relationships are the central focus.

Research on the treatment of depression has a history of a little over thirty years. During that time the field has advanced by the development of standard therapy manuals and workbooks for depression. In most cases an individual psychologist or psychiatrist has developed a theoretical view of depression and has written a therapy manual to allow other therapists to apply the same therapy methods. These standardized therapies have then been reliably evaluated. Research into the theory that underlies the therapy often follows the therapy evaluations. The book you are about to read comes from a very different approach. In this instance, rather than beginning with theory, the authors draw on a considerable body of research on the interpersonal nature of depression. They have integrated this research into a systematic series of steps to take that will lead down a path to overcome depression.

Thomas Joiner and his colleagues and students, including Jeremy Pettit, have been leaders in studying the interpersonal behavior of people when they are depressed for a number of years. They have studied the interpersonal strategies and motives of depressed and non-depressed individuals and extracted a view of how depressed people typically operate with others. They are thus in a position to draw on their research findings and translate them into practical suggestions for readers to use.

Pettit and Joiner have translated the essential conclusions of their research into easily accessible language and practical exercises and activities for the non-professional reader. You will find this workbook interactive in the sense that it asks you questions in order to determine how the ideas presented may apply to you. The authors take you through rationale and evidence to practical suggestions for application. Readers who suffer from depression, and concerned friends and relatives who may read this book, will find much of value in the book's helpful applications based on solid research evidence.

—Lynn P. Rehm, Ph.D. ABPP
Department of Psychology,
University of Houston

Acknowledgments

There are many individuals who have contributed to the development of this book, either directly or indirectly. We are indebted to our mentors, colleagues, and students, who have refined our understanding of depression and encourage us to continue expanding our knowledge of this disorder. We also wish to express our gratitude to Catharine Sutker and the staff at New Harbinger Publications for their initial belief in the project and support of it through its completion. Above all, we are grateful to our patients, who have allowed us to observe, learn from, and support them in their battles with depression.

Introduction

This book is based upon the premise that depression develops and is sustained, at least in part, by interpersonal processes and that intervening in these processes can help relieve depression. Hence, we've written this book with two goals in mind. The first goal is to enhance your awareness of the role that interpersonal behaviors play in promoting and maintaining your depression. The second, related goal is to spell out concrete strategies for changing how you interact with others in a way that will reduce your depression (and improve your interpersonal relationships). To these ends, we draw upon current scientific knowledge of the patterns of interpersonal behaviors at work in depression, as well as how changing these behavioral patterns may reduce depressive experiences.

Before proceeding, let us clarify what we mean by "interpersonal behaviors." This term simply refers to the things you say and do to communicate with other people. Importantly, this term includes both intentional efforts to express something to others, such as asking your friend if she would like to see a movie, and unintentional actions that may send messages to others, like how often you touch your face when speaking with a coworker. That is, at times you are very aware of the things you do in social interactions; other behaviors, however, slip below your radar because they are inconspicuous or because you've done them so many times that they now seem automatic. Interpersonal behaviors include all of these instances.

As you have probably noticed from watching television, surfing the Internet, or perusing the self-help section at your local bookstore, many treatments are available for depression.

Those that do not take into consideration the impact of depression on interpersonal relationships, and the impact that relationships have on depression, are often unsuccessful or only partially successful. In our opinion, this is because it is impossible to tease apart the experience of depression from the interpersonal context in which it occurs. Treatments that do not directly address interpersonal contexts may help you feel better for short periods of time, but to the extent that your social environment influences depression, your symptoms are likely to reappear if the interpersonal context stays the same.

When these kinds of treatments do produce lasting improvement, we suspect that this is due in part to their indirect influence on interpersonal behaviors. For example, antidepressant medications may lead to improvements in mood, energy, and motivation, which in turn may bring about more positive social behaviors and interactions. In this sense, treatments that do not focus on interpersonal behaviors may reduce depression over longer periods of time because they indirectly lead to positive changes in your relationships with other people.

The primary goal of this book is to teach you how to identify—and, more importantly, modify—common interpersonal behaviors that cause your depression or make it worse.

WHO IS THIS BOOK FOR?

This book is for anyone who experiences frequent periods of depressed mood. If you have depressive symptoms that are severe enough to warrant a diagnosis of major depressive disorder or dysthymic disorder (see chapter 1), you will likely find this book most helpful. However, even if your symptoms are less intense or don't last as long, you are also likely to benefit from the principles we discuss in this book. The same types of interpersonal behavior patterns are at work; the difference may simply be a matter of degree or pervasiveness of these behaviors. If you suffer from periods of depressed mood, we encourage you to consider how the strategies we teach in this book may improve the quality of your life.

The majority of the research findings that led to the development of this book came from studies of people with symptoms of *unipolar depression* (that is, major depression and dysthymia). Unfortunately, less is known about the role of interpersonal behaviors in *bipolar disorder* (periods of depressed mood alternating with periods of extremely elevated mood, high energy, and decreased need for sleep; formerly called "manic depression"). While we think it likely that some of the behaviors that contribute to depression operate similarly during the depressed phases of bipolar disorder, interpersonal behaviors that occur during the manic phases of bipolar disorder probably differ greatly. Hence, if you have bipolar disorder, you may benefit from the strategies in this book that seem most relevant to your experience, but you should keep in mind that the applicability of these principles to bipolar disorder hasn't yet been investigated scientifically.

This book may also be helpful for your friends and family members. As we'll demonstrate throughout the course of this book, depression occurs within the social context in which you live and operate on a daily basis. This interpersonal context can include family members, friends, coworkers, and your spouse or romantic partner, as well as the way that you interact with them. It is important to recognize that your depression affects the way you think and feel and the way you communicate with other people. Because it affects your communication, your depression also influences the way others think and feel and the way others communicate with you. As your friends and family develop a greater understanding of how depressed people behave, as well as how these behaviors can make depression more chronic, they may be better prepared to empathize with you and assist you in your recovery.

The primary value of an interpersonal approach to treating depression is that it leads to changes in both your actions and the actions of those around you. In contrast to other treatment approaches that focus on how you interpret situations or how events in your childhood may influence your depression, an interpersonal approach encourages you to actively change your current relationships with other people. This approach is based upon the notion that any change in the way you communicate with others necessitates a change in their reaction. For example, your friends are likely to respond very differently to you if you come across as sullen and grumpy, on the one hand, or if you come across as upbeat and cheerful, on the other. In this sense, *you* can become an active agent of change in your social environment. By changing how you interact, you will change how you feel, how others feel when they're around you, and how others interact with you. As others notice your changes and become more positive in their relationships with you, you will continue to feel even better.

Finally, we wish to point out that you may use this workbook alone or in conjunction with other forms of treatment, such as antidepressant medications or regular visits to a therapist or counselor.

HOW IS THIS BOOK LAID OUT?

We begin with a general discussion of depression in chapter 1, including its symptoms, prevalence, and possible causes. There is a section in the chapter that will allow you to evaluate your own depressive symptoms. In the latter portion of chapter 1, we present an overview of research linking depression and interpersonal relationships.

Subsequent chapters expand upon this overview and focus in depth on specific interpersonal problem areas and strategies for interacting in ways that will improve both your depression and your relationships. Because chapters 2 through 8 each address a particular aspect of interpersonal functioning, you may wish to skip around from chapter to chapter as you deem the topics relevant to your own personal experiences. Nevertheless, we have organized the chapters in a logical sequence, and we encourage you to read this book in order. In chapter 9, we tie together the material presented in all of the earlier chapters into an integrated review. Regardless of the order in which you read chapters 2 through 8, we strongly recommend that you read each of these chapters before reading chapter 9.

The book is organized in a workbook format with exercises, checklists, and practice materials. These exercises will help you identify and change interpersonal behaviors that might be aggravating your depressive experiences. We encourage you to make copies of them for your own personal use. You'll probably notice that the more actively and consistently you engage in the strategies and exercises presented in this book, the more improvement you will notice in your depression and in your interactions with others. Although it is now cliché, the idea that you get out what you put in is particularly relevant here.

WHEN TO SEEK PROFESSIONAL HELP

As we mentioned earlier, this book is designed to be used either alone or in conjunction with formal treatment. However, if you think that your symptoms meet the diagnostic criteria for major depression or dysthymia (exercises 1.1 and 1.2 will help you determine this), we encourage you to also consider treatment from a mental health professional. Whether or not you are already in treatment, if your depressive symptoms worsen to the point that you repeatedly think about dying or harming yourself, it is very important to discuss this with your treatment provider or to seek out professional help if you are not already in treatment.

A WORD OF ENCOURAGEMENT

Before you begin practicing the strategies we discuss, we feel compelled to mention a few potential stumbling blocks in your path to improvement. First, you may find it difficult to carry through with the exercises. This is not because they are excessively time-consuming or complicated; in fact, they are quite straightforward. Rather, you may find certain exercises challenging because they require you to change long-standing (although unhealthy) patterns of interacting with others. Given that over a period of years you have probably developed a relatively consistent style of relating to others, it will likely take hard work and continued effort to change these habits. We encourage you to keep at it. With time and consistent practice, new and healthier interpersonal behaviors will become automatic, so that you will no longer feel as though you are constantly working to change.

There might be times when you feel like you are faking behaviors or acting in ways that just don't seem like the "real you." Once again, this is because you have developed particular ways of interacting with other people over many years, and any sudden change to those methods can feel unusual or inconsistent with how you view yourself. However, to the extent that your interpersonal habits contribute to your feelings of depression, it is in your best interest to consider changing them. What's more, the behaviors that may initially feel fake will soon begin to feel quite comfortable as your depression symptoms improve. In *Hamlet*, Shakespeare wrote, "Assume a virtue, if you have it not . . . for use can almost change the stamp of nature" (1998, 70), and we think he was right.

Finally, as you start the process of altering certain interpersonal behaviors, keep in mind that any changes you make will influence not only you but also those with whom you interact—especially close friends, coworkers, and family members. (We return to this point in chapters 8 and 9.) As a rule, the strategies outlined in this book will bring about positive interpersonal experiences. However, other people may initially react with surprise, indifference, or even resistance to your changes. Remember that they too have grown accustomed to your typical way of interacting with them, so they will also need time to adjust to your new behavioral repertoire. We again encourage you to keep at it, because the long-term benefits of healthier ways of interacting far outweigh the costs of those changes.

Depression: An Interpersonal Problem

In this chapter, we define the different types of depression and guide you in understanding your own experience of depression. We talk about the prevalence of depression and look at its possible causes, including our focus in this book: interpersonal behaviors.

WHAT IS DEPRESSION?

Let's begin by developing a clearer understanding of what depression is. The current diagnostic scheme used by the vast majority of mental health professionals, the *Diagnostic and Statistical Manual of Mental Disorders* (DSM), describes several forms of depression. We focus on two of those, major depression and dysthymia, as well as one form that is not yet in the DSM, double depression. While bipolar disorders include other forms of depression, we will not emphasize them here.

Major Depression

Major depression is a condition that persists, causes distress or impairment, and involves certain symptom patterns. We address each of these three in turn.

First, major depression is relatively persistent. By definition, the symptoms that constitute major depression must be present more days than not for at least two weeks. Major depression is generally a chronic condition. Its course is both *episodic* (intermittent) and recurrent. As you may have experienced, the disorder comes and goes. At times, it is in full swing, with numerous and severe symptoms; at other times, it is mild or moderate, with symptoms present but less noticeable; at still other times, it is absent, with symptoms in full remission.

Second, the symptoms of major depression cause significant distress and impairment. That is, they are disturbing, unpleasant, or painful. The symptoms may also hinder your ability to effectively function at work, school, or in other settings.

Third, major depression includes a majority of the following symptoms:

- sadness

- loss of capacity for pleasure *(anhedonia)*

- low energy

- suicidal thoughts or behaviors

- difficulty falling asleep, staying asleep, or getting up in the morning

- changes in appetite, gaining or losing weight without trying

- *psychomotor disturbance* (slowing or agitation)

- difficulty concentrating

- feelings of guilt or worthlessness

Dysthymia

Another form of depression, *dysthymia*, is more constant and chronic than major depression. Dysthymia may be viewed as a low-grade, persistent version of major depression. It is defined as a depressed mood that has persisted for most of the day for more days than not over the course of at least two years. In addition to depressed mood, at least two of the following symptoms must be present for a diagnosis of dysthymia:

- low energy

- difficulty falling asleep, staying asleep, or getting up in the morning

- changes in appetite, gaining or losing weight without trying

- difficulty concentrating

- low self-esteem

■ feelings of hopelessness

While diagnostic criteria state that symptoms must be present for at least two years, the reality is that quite a few people experience the symptoms of dysthymia for many years. Because dysthymia can last so long, you can come to view the symptoms as a normal part of your personality. Be assured that they are not.

Double Depression

A third form of depression, *double depression,* involves major depression superimposed on dysthymia. For example, consider a woman who has had depressed mood more days than not for around four years, accompanied by energy and concentration problems. On the basis of these symptoms and their duration, we can conclude that she has dysthymia. Suddenly, her symptoms become much more severe and expand to include sleep and appetite disturbance, suicidal thoughts, and restlessness. In this case, a major depression has developed on top of the dysthymia.

Double depression is not a formal term in the DSM, but is worth noting for a couple of reasons. First, it entails both severe symptoms (major depression) and chronic symptoms (dysthymia). Consequently, it is a quite debilitating form of depression. Second, research suggests that people with double depression may respond to treatment more slowly than those with major depression or dysthymia alone, although this isn't always the case (Amore and Jori 2001).

UNDERSTANDING YOUR DEPRESSION

As you can see, depression is characterized by a range of symptoms, in contrast to the common misperception that depression simply refers to feeling sad or blue. In fact, the experience of depression is quite varied—well over two hundred different combinations of symptoms all satisfy the current definition of major depression (Buchwald and Rudick-Davis 1993). In this section, you have the opportunity to examine the depressive symptoms you may be experiencing. While we encourage you to seek formal evaluation from a mental health professional rather than attempting to diagnose yourself, the self-assessments in this chapter may help you better understand the nature, severity, and duration of your symptoms.

Your Depression Symptoms

Let's begin by taking a look at your symptoms.

EXERCISE 1.1:   Assessing the Symptoms of Your Depression

This exercise will help you identify which—and how many—symptoms you are currently experiencing. Below is a list of the nine symptom criteria used to establish a diagnosis of major depression, as well as a description of each symptom. Check the appropriate box if you experience a particular symptom more days than not. Next, add up the total number of checked boxes and enter your score at the bottom.

Check if present
more days than not

1. Depressed mood or sadness   ☐
    You may feel sad or like you have the blues.

2. Loss of interest or inability to experience pleasure   ☐
    Things that were fun or interesting in the past no longer seem pleasurable, and
    you may even have stopped doing them altogether.

3. Changes in appetite or weight   ☐
    You may have noticed a relatively sudden increase or decrease in your appetite.
    Similarly, you may lost or gained weight even though you were not actively trying
    to do so.

4. Sleep disturbance   ☐
    You might have difficulty falling asleep or staying asleep, or you might wake up in
    the middle of the night or unusually early in the morning and not be able to fall
    asleep again. Or you may sleep more than you used to and have more difficulty
    than usual getting out of bed in the morning.

5. Restlessness or sluggishness   ☐
    You may feel on edge, fidgety, or unable to sit still. Or you may feel slowed down
    or lethargic—so much so that your arms and legs feel heavy and difficult to move.

6. Fatigue or loss of energy   ☐
    You may have frequent feelings of tiredness and lack of energy.

7. Feelings of worthlessness or guilt   ☐
    You may have low self-esteem, such that you feel of no value. You may also have
    excessive feelings of guilt, beyond what most people would experience in response
    to negative events.

8. Difficulty concentrating or making decisions   ☐
    It may feel hard to focus on tasks at hand and concentrate without your mind drifting
    to other topics (often sad topics). It may also be hard to make even minor decisions,
    such as what clothes to wear or what to eat for dinner.

9. Thoughts of death or suicide   ☐
    You may think a lot about death in general or have thoughts about what it would be
    like to die, who would come to your funeral, and so on. You may even wish that you
    were dead or think of ending your life.

    Total score (number of checked boxes):   _____

If your total score is less than three, then you are not currently experiencing an episode of
major depression or dysthymia. Your depressive symptoms, if any, are considered *subsyndromal,*
or minor, because you do not meet the diagnostic criteria for a depressive disorder.

If your total score is five or greater, and you checked box one or box two (or both), then
you are experiencing symptoms that are consistent with major depression. If your total score is
between three and five, and you checked "depressed mood or sadness" but not "thoughts of
death or suicide," then you are experiencing symptoms consistent with dysthymia.

Your Depression over Time

Remember that your combination of symptoms is only one component to understanding
the scope of your depression. The duration of your symptoms must also be considered. Depression is often a chronic condition, and there are three aspects of your experience of depression
over time: episode duration, recurrence, and relapse.

EPISODE DURATION

Episode duration has to do with the fact that depression lasts so long. On average, major
depression lasts around eight months in adults and may last even longer in youth (American
Psychiatric Association 1994). These long episodes involve prolonged experience of the most
acute, painful, and debilitating aspects of depression.

It is worth dwelling on this point. There are other acutely painful conditions (for example,
stomach flu), but there are few that are acutely painful for such a long period of time. The
stomach flu typically goes away in three days or so. Several months is the average episode
length; if you experience longer than average episodes, you may face years of suffering and
impairment.

The story with dysthymia is equally astounding. What dysthymia lacks in acute pain (remember that it's a low-grade form of depression) it makes up for in sheer length of episodes. The average length of dysthymic episodes is around a decade, and it is relatively common for people in their forties and older to report decades-long dysthymias. For example, a woman in her fifties who has experienced persistent, low-grade depressive symptoms since her teens has had a forty-year episode.

Clearly, episode length or duration is important in how you experience depression over time. Once depression finally does go away, it tends to return. The two other important aspects of the timeline of depression have to do with its return.

RECURRENCE

Recurrence is defined as the return of clinical depression following a symptom-free period. Someone who recovers fully from a past depression but then experiences another episode of depression can be said to have experienced a recurrence. Recurrence, too, is important in that it can affect substantial portions of your life.

RELAPSE

There are times when people get somewhat better from a past depression, but some depressive symptoms remain nonetheless. Someone who partially recovers from a past depression but then experiences another depression is said to have experienced a relapse. *Relapse* is the resumption of symptoms in the vulnerable time frame just following remission of a depressive episode. Like recurrence and episode duration, relapse conveys the chronic nature of depression.

There is an important distinction among episode duration, recurrence, and relapse. If you are experiencing a long-lasting episode, depressive symptoms are an obvious part of the clinical picture. So, too, with relapse: you have partially recovered, but depressive symptoms remain. In both of these cases, depressive symptoms are part of the picture. Depression recurrence, however, is different. By definition, recurrence includes a period of time when you have fully recovered and do not meet the diagnostic criteria for major depression. The importance of this distinction to you is that the absence of symptoms right now does not necessarily mean you can't become depressed again in the future. In fact, we believe that there is a good chance you will continue to be at risk for depression until you change your patterns of interacting with other people.

As an aside, we realize that you may be feeling demoralized now that you've read about how chronic depression can be and how it tends to recur. Indeed, this is a sobering aspect of depression and is not to be taken lightly. But we encourage you to hang in there and stick with the material outlined in this book, because depression does not have to consume vast portions of your life. By using the strategies present in this book, you can significantly reduce and even put an end to long-standing bouts of depression.

Let's take a look at how chronic, or long-standing, your depression is.

EXERCISE 1.2:   Assessing the Duration of Your Depression

For how long have the symptoms you checked in exercise 1.1 been present?

☐   A day or two

☐   Several days, but less than two weeks

☐   A few weeks (at least two)

☐   Several months

☐   Several years (two or more)

☐   As long as you can remember

Diagnostic *Criteria*

Now that you have examined the severity and duration of your symptoms, let's return to the issue of diagnostic criteria.

MAJOR DEPRESSION

If you checked at least five symptoms in exercise 1.1, including "depressed mood or sadness," "loss of interest or inability to experience pleasure," or both, and they have been present more days than not for at least two weeks, then you may be experiencing a major depressive episode. If your symptoms have been present for less than two weeks, then you do not yet meet diagnostic criteria for major depression, although you might soon if your symptoms persist.

DYSTHYMIA

If you checked between three and five symptoms in exercise 1.1 and your symptoms have been present for two years or longer, then you are likely experiencing dysthymia. Recall that this is a more chronic, low-grade form of depression.

DOUBLE DEPRESSION

If you checked at least five current symptoms and you have experienced low-grade symptoms for two years or more, then you may be experiencing double depression. Remember that double depression doesn't mean that you are twice as depressed as others; rather, it indicates major depression on top of ongoing dysthymia. This form of depression is both severe and chronic, and it may respond more slowly to treatment. We don't mean to discourage you if you have these symptoms. Instead, we mention this to let you know that it may take a little extra time, work, and practice to improve your depression.

MINOR DEPRESSION

Even if you don't meet the diagnostic criteria for major depression, dysthymia, or double depression (perhaps you don't have a sufficient number of symptoms or the symptoms don't last long enough), but you do experience some symptoms, we still encourage you to learn the strategies outlined in this book. We make this recommendation because research demonstrates that people with minor depression have similar problems in interpersonal functioning (Lewinsohn et al. 2000).

Comparing Courses and Severity Levels

Figure 1.1 is a sample representation of the typical number of symptoms and duration of major depression, dysthymia, double depression, and minor depression over a two-year period. Note that this graph is just an example, so the course of your symptoms likely differs somewhat from any of the four courses showed here. As you can see in the graph, the different types of depression have different courses over time and different levels of severity. We list some of their features below.

Major depression has an episodic course, going from *subclinical* levels (less than five symptoms) up to between five and eight depressive symptoms, then returning to subclinical levels. This all occurs within the two-year period, and the major depressive episode lasts for less than one year.

Dysthymia has a stable course, marked by the presence of three or four depressive symptoms that change very little during the two-year period.

Double depression has an episodic course, but at least three depressive symptoms are always present during the two years. For some of the time, the symptom level reaches the range of major depression (that is, more than five symptoms).

Minor depression can be somewhat episodic, but there are never five or more symptoms present for two weeks or more.

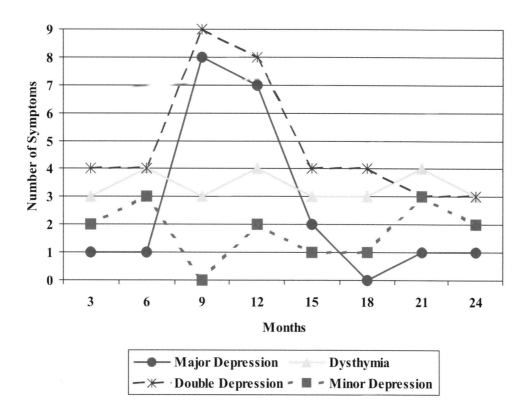

Figure 1.1: Examples of Courses and Severity Levels

EXERCISE 1.3: Assessing the Course and Severity Level of Your Depression

In the following blank graph, chart the progression of your symptoms over the previous two years, to the best of your recollection. You can refer to the list of symptoms in exercise 1.1. Although you may find it hard to remember exactly when you experienced particular symptoms, we encourage you to try your best to establish a timeline of your depressive symptom level.

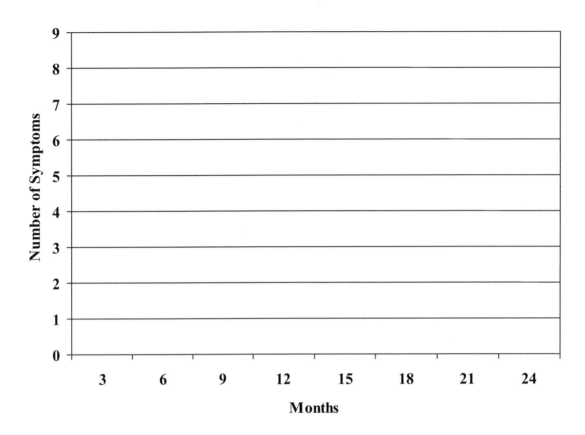

If the exercises in this chapter lead you to believe that you may be experiencing some form of depression, we recommend that you confirm this impression with a mental health professional or a physician.

HOW PREVALENT IS DEPRESSION?

If you are experiencing depressive symptoms, either major or minor, you are far from alone. Very far, in fact. At any given time, between 4 and 10 percent of the U.S. population is experiencing major depression or dysthymia, and between 15 and 20 percent have experienced major depression or dysthymia at some point in their lives. Another 4 percent experience minor depressive symptoms at any given time but don't meet full criteria for a diagnosis (Judd, Akiskal, and Paulus 1997). Because of its high prevalence, depression is often referred to as the common cold of mental illness. However, the fact that depression is common by no means suggests that it is not serious or painful. If you have ever had the flu, you can attest to the fact that the flu's widespread nature does not diminish the severity of its symptoms.

An aspect of depression prevalence has concerned researchers and mental health professionals in recent years. It appears as though an enormously important age-related phenomenon may be occurring. If, in the early 2000s, you are about seventy years old, the chance that you have experienced depression in your lifetime is about 2 percent. If, in the early 2000s, you are in your fifties, your lifetime chance of depression is approximately 5 percent. Despite fewer years in which to get depressed, this younger group is nonetheless about twice as likely to have experienced depression. This is remarkable enough, but astoundingly, the same pattern continues in younger and younger groups. Those in their thirties in the late 1990s have approximately an 8 percent risk of lifetime depression; teenagers in the late 1990s, despite approximately four times fewer years than their seventy-year-old counterparts, experience approximately six times more risk for lifetime depression (Seligman 1998). If this trend continues, imagine the rates when these teenagers reach late life.

Apparently, depression is on the rise. Why? One possibility is that the trend is artificial and not really representative of a true increase in depression over time. For example, perhaps the older you get, the more prone you are to forget having experienced a prior depression. Or perhaps health-care professionals are doing an increasingly better job of detecting depression; if so, what has changed is the behavior of health professionals, not the rates of depression. Or perhaps it is increasingly acceptable to report depression. If so, what has changed is the perceived stigma of depression, rather than the actual rates of depression.

But if increased prevalence were merely due to forgetting, why would thirty-year-olds differ so much from eighteen-year-olds? Also, we could only wish that depression were stigma free or that health-care professionals detect it carefully. Although there has been progress on both these fronts, there has not been so much progress as to account for the large difference in rates. The increase in prevalence rates thus appears to be a real phenomenon.

Why might depression be on the increase? Many possible explanations exist, including changes in environmental toxins, increased drug abuse, and changes in parenting practices, but none yet has good scientific backing. Perhaps the increasing prevalence of depression is due to an escalation in general causes of depression, which we discuss next.

POSSIBLE CAUSES OF DEPRESSION

In these times of mass media outlets like television, radio, and particularly the Internet, you have probably heard several theories—all with "expert" support—on the causes of depression. The causes are no doubt many. In fact, most depression researchers long ago dismissed the notion that depression had one and only one cause. A more current understanding is that multiple pathways lead to depression, and these pathways likely interact with each other to produce the symptoms that you experience.

In this section, we very briefly review some general factors that likely play a role in the development of depression. This is by no means a review of all possible causes of depression;

rather, it is a quick overview of general causes before we discuss interpersonal behaviors and depression.

Genetic and Biological

If you have heard some of the claims made about what causes depression, then you have no doubt heard arguments that your genes play a role in determining whether or not you experience depression. Indeed, evidence does suggest a genetic link to depression, although it would be an overstatement to claim that depression is entirely determined by our genetic makeup. The fact that depression tends to run in families supports a genetic component to depression. Interestingly, the greater the level of genetic overlap (for example, brother or sister as compared to cousin), the greater the likelihood that two people will both have depression or neither have depression.

That evidence, while important, isn't particularly compelling because close relatives are also more likely to live in similar environments. As a result, their overlap in depression could be the result of shared environmental factors (such as poverty, death of an immediate family member, or strained relations between family members). Stronger evidence for a genetic component of depression comes from studies that have examined the rates of depression among biological relatives who have been adopted into different homes, as well as from comparisons of twins with other close relatives. Based on these types of studies, estimates suggest that having a close relative with depression makes you two to three times more likely to experience depression (Sullivan, Neale, and Kendler 2000). Ongoing research seeks to identify specific genes that may be implicated in depression, but consistent findings have yet to emerge.

In addition to genetic contributions, biological systems clearly play a role in depression. Although the mechanism is not yet well understood, *neurotransmitters* (chemical messengers in the brain) such as serotonin, norepinephrine, and dopamine all appear to be related to mood and, consequently, depression. Popular antidepressant medications like Prozac (fluoxetine) and Zoloft (sertraline) influence these neurotransmitter systems.

Psychological

Many psychological factors have been linked to the development of depression. In particular, stressful life events—and more importantly, your interpretations of these events—may be causal factors for depression. Stressful events (such as the loss of a job, the ending of a romantic relationship, or failure at school), when combined with a tendency to view them as outside of your control, to repeatedly turn them over in your mind, and to develop a hopeless outlook toward life, greatly increase the likelihood of depression. Moreover, as depressive symptoms develop, people often tend to form negative views about themselves, their environment, and their future (Beck 1976), increasing the likelihood that they will continue to feel depressed.

Interpersonal

There is no doubt that humans are social creatures. Across virtually all areas of physical and mental health, evidence is emerging to suggest that interpersonal relations play an important role in positive—and negative—outcomes. Depression is no exception. Throughout this book, we emphasize the role of interpersonal functioning in causing and reinforcing depressive symptoms. Your interpersonal context greatly influences whether you become depressed, your subjective experience of depression, the ways in which you show depression, and the resolution of your depressive symptoms.

In each of the next seven chapters, we highlight a specific aspect of interpersonal functioning. First, however, we'll provide a broader overview of research suggesting a link between interpersonal behaviors and depression.

HOW DEPRESSION WORKS IN RELATIONSHIPS

In general, people who suffer from depression tend to experience pervasive difficulties in interpersonal relationships, be it with their spouses or significant others, bosses or coworkers, or even with unfamiliar people they encounter in the course of a normal day (for example, in the checkout line at a grocery store). Research indicates that depressed people tend to be dissatisfied with both the quality and the quantity of their relationships (Segrin 2000). They report more relationship conflict, more arguing with family members and significant others, and less support from others, and they are more likely to feel lonely than people who are not depressed. Moreover, and perhaps as a result of these factors, depressed people often withdraw from social relationships. Research suggests that depressed people are more likely to be shy, more passive in interpersonal settings, and more dependent upon others to make decisions for them (Segrin 2000).

In addition to having more relationship conflict and dissatisfaction, people are often less effective in interpersonal relationships when they are depressed. That is, when they interact with others, they are less likely to get what they want out of the interaction. This can be because depression is often accompanied by tendencies toward unassertiveness and avoidance of interpersonal conflict, as well as difficulty connecting with others. For example, people who are depressed may fail to make eye contact, smile infrequently, keep their head down, or speak slowly and in a monotone. When this occurs, it can have the unintended consequence of conveying a lack of interest in social interactions. The key word here is "unintended;" people who are depressed clearly desire good relationships with others. Unfortunately, some of the symptoms of depression interfere with the process of developing and maintaining healthy relationships.

Another example of the way depression interferes with relationships is seen in the things depressed people say: they tend to talk more about topics that have a negative theme. This drift toward negativity even extends to making disparaging or belittling comments about themselves.

Depressed people—and those at risk for becoming depressed—also communicate in ways that may have the unintended consequence of actually promoting unfriendly reactions, or at times even rejection, from others. People who are depressed tend to request or show preferences for negative evaluations from others. It is not that people like negative evaluations—in fact, such responses are understandably quite upsetting. Nevertheless, negative appraisals are more readily accepted because they are consistent with the negative self-concept that many depressed people hold. You may dismiss positive appraisals if the appraisals don't match your (largely negative) self-concept. Let us be clear again that it is not that people who are depressed enjoy negative evaluations from others; rather, it is difficult to accept positive comments from others while simultaneously holding a negative view of yourself. Remember that one of the primary symptoms of depression is feelings of worthlessness or excessive guilt.

At the same time, and perhaps in an effort to relieve the feelings of worthlessness, depressed people often ask for assurances from others that they are valuable and likable. That in and of itself is not harmful, and it is something that virtually everybody (depressed or not) does; the problem is that depression tends to turn up the volume. In other words, requests for comfort and assurance increase during periods of depression and can become excessive at times. This is a natural response to the symptoms of depression. Depression is characterized by feelings of low self-worth, and asking for others to affirm that you are a good, likeable person is one way of overcoming these feelings. As we discuss in chapter 7, however, this process can damage your relationships.

As a prelude to chapters 6 and 7, consider the following scenario. Jill has been depressed for some time now, feels frustrated with herself and down on herself for being depressed, and believes that nothing she does turns out right. While talking with her husband one evening, she asks him the following:

Jill:	Do you still like me, you know, as a person?
John:	What do you mean? Of course I like you. I love you.
Jill:	Yeah, but all I do is cry all day, and I can't even do little things right anymore. Like yesterday, when I forgot to call the restaurant ahead of time to make a reservation.
John:	I know you've been feeling badly lately and struggling with things, but that doesn't change how I feel about you. I still like you.
Jill:	Come on, I could tell that you got mad about the restaurant thing last night.
John:	Well, yeah, I was upset at the time, but like I told you, I still like you and love you.
Jill:	You don't have to be nice just to keep from hurting my feelings. Admit it—you're tired of me and sick of putting up with my mistakes.
John:	*(getting frustrated and raising his voice)* What are you talking about? What else do I have to do for you to believe me when I say that I like you?
Jill:	See, you're getting angry at me again. I knew you didn't really like me anymore.

Jill's feelings of worthlessness led her to ask her husband for reassurance that he still likes her. His assurance, however, didn't fit with Jill's view of herself as worthless, and so it was difficult for her to accept. As a result, she pushed him harder and eventually began pressing him to tell her that he really didn't like her. Unfortunately, this had the unintended consequence of leaving her husband frustrated. It is important to emphasize here that Jill did not set out to exasperate her husband; rather, she desired comfort from him and closeness with him. Part of the vicious nature of depression is that it can lead to these kinds of exchanges, which obviously place a strain on relationships. The depressed person leaves the conversation feeling just as bad as before, or even worse, and the other person leaves the interaction feeling frustrated and confused by not being able to comfort the depressed companion.

If you identify with some of the behaviors we have described in this section, don't be discouraged. The good news is that these behaviors are just that: behaviors. They are not personality traits or characteristics of the "real you." As such, they can be changed to produce more positive outcomes. By systematically following the exercises in this book, you will change these behaviors, and in so doing, you will become less depressed and improve your relationships with others.

PUTTING IT ALL TOGETHER

Thus far, we have described some general causes of depression, including genetic, biological, psychological, and interpersonal factors. In reality, however, depression results from the interplay of all these areas. It would be overly simplistic to view depression as the result of only biological or only psychological factors, because these areas overlap and influence one another. The questions listed below will help you consider what areas in your life might contribute to your experience of depression.

EXERCISE 1.4: A Look Back

Does depression, or related conditions like anxiety or substance use problems, run in your family? How many relatives do you know of with problems in these areas, and how closely related to you are they?

_____

_____

_____

Have you recently experienced a lot of stress? List specific sources of stress in your life and rate them on a scale from 1 (not at all stressful) to 10 (extremely stressful).

_____

_____

_____

What is your typical way of responding to these stressors?

_____

_____

_____

What other areas do you think might influence your depressive symptoms?

_____

_____

_____

List the most important people in your life, whether your relationship is positive or negative. For each, describe what you get out of the relationship. Beside each name, rate your overall satisfaction with the quality of that relationship on a scale from 1 (very dissatisfied) to 10 (very satisfied).

_____

_____

_____

_____

_____

_____

OUR APPROACH

While taking other factors into account, we will focus primarily on interpersonal behaviors that lead to and maintain depression, because we believe that changing how you relate to others is often sufficient—and at times necessary—to improve depression. However, we want to make it clear that we do not view changing your interpersonal style as the only route to feeling better. Indeed, biological treatment (such as antidepressant medications) and psychological treatment (such as cognitive therapy) can be quite effective, and we encourage you to also consider those methods of treating your depression. Likewise, our approach is not mutually exclusive with other forms of treatment. You could simultaneously take antidepressant medications under the care of a physician and use this book on your own. Having said that, we firmly believe that the principles in this book, when routinely and systematically practiced, will help you improve your mood and relationships.

LOOKING AHEAD

In the following chapters, we discuss in more detail the ways that depressed people typically relate to others. We challenge you with exercises that will help you put a stop to those behaviors that maintain or exacerbate your depression and help you develop healthier patterns of interacting.

In chapter 2, we cover the "how," "what," and "with whom" of interpersonal behaviors that are typical of people with depression, and we challenge you to carefully monitor your own patterns of communicating with others. We emphasize both verbal and nonverbal communication.

In chapter 3, we discuss in greater detail social skills among depressed people, including their views of themselves and others' views of their social skills. We challenge you to develop a more accurate view of your social skills by collecting data on your social skills in actual interactions, and then challenge you to test your perhaps long-held beliefs about your ability to effectively interact in social settings.

In chapter 4, we discuss the roles of shyness, loneliness, and conflict avoidance in depression, and we challenge you to overcome your inhibitions by becoming more assertive.

Chapter 5 presents an overview of *self-handicapping*, or selling yourself short to others. Your challenge will be to confront the fear of failure and negative evaluation by putting yourself out on a limb and not publicly underestimating your abilities.

In chapter 6, we cover the interpersonal behavior of negative feedback seeking, and discuss why depressed people ask for negative evaluations. We challenge you to change the mental filter that may lead you to reject positive feedback and solicit negative feedback.

Chapter 7 addresses the problems of excessive dependence on others and continually seeking reassurance from others. We challenge you to become aware of your own reassurance-seeking behaviors, to test the beliefs underlying your desire for reassurance, and then to focus greater portions of your social interactions on others rather than on yourself.

In chapter 8, we discuss depression in the context of family relations and the impact that depressive interpersonal behaviors can have on spouses and children. We challenge you to work toward increasing family cohesion, primarily by applying the strategies discussed in chapters 2 through 7 to your home environment.

Finally, chapter 9 reviews and integrates the material in chapters 2 through 8. We encourage you to examine how changing one set of interpersonal behaviors will often lead to changes in another set of behaviors. We also provide some suggestions and words of encouragement about dealing with potential setbacks, including resistance to change from others.

2

It's Not Just What You Say but Also How You Say It

In chapter 1, we provided an overview of the symptoms and forms of depression. In this chapter, we highlight the interpersonal behaviors of depressed people, paying particular attention to two different types of communication: verbal and nonverbal.

INTERPERSONAL BEHAVIORS OF DEPRESSED PEOPLE

We all establish patterns, or styles, of interacting with others in our environment. Certainly, our specific interpersonal styles differ depending upon the particular person with whom we interact and the setting. For example, the content of your speech, as well as your nonverbal behaviors such as body posture, eye contact, and rate of speech, may differ drastically between a yearly evaluation meeting with a supervisor, on the one hand, and a conversation with a close friend while eating pizza and watching TV, on the other.

While this sort of variation in interpersonal styles is perfectly natural, people who are depressed tend to show a set of common, identifiable interpersonal behaviors. That is, there are certain communication styles and behaviors seen among depressed people that are not typically seen among others. What's more, some of these patterns tend to occur only when somebody is depressed and then virtually disappear as the depression lifts. Other communication styles appear more stable, regardless of the level of depression experienced.

Some of these behaviors are quite obvious to yourself and to others, whereas other behaviors may fly beneath your radar; that is, you may not realize that you do them. Most people have a general sense—accurate or not—of how depressed people act in social settings. These perceptions are likely influenced by watching or interacting with other people who are depressed or by media portrayals of depressed people.

EXERCISE 2.1: How Do Depressed People Act in Social Situations?

In the space provided below, describe some interpersonal behaviors that you have noticed in depressed people in general (not necessarily in yourself). Examples to help you get started are *They don't talk much, They don't make eye contact,* and so on. These will likely be more obvious, rather than subtle, behaviors.

_____

_____

_____

_____

Now that you have described some common interpersonal behaviors of depressed people in general, let's make it more personal.

EXERCISE 2.2: How Do You Act in Social Situations When You Are Depressed?

Below, describe behaviors that you notice in *yourself* when you feel depressed. For example, you might list *I avoid looking directly at people* or *I don't smile* if those are things you do when you are depressed. Remember, the goal here is not to list stereotypical behaviors of all depressed people but rather to describe the specific ways that you interact with others when you are depressed. Clearly, there may be some overlap, but try to pinpoint the features that best characterize your style when you are depressed.

As the last step in this set of exercises, let's look at how your behavior is different when you're not depressed.

EXERCISE 2.3:   How Do Your Interpersonal Behaviors When You Are Depressed Differ from When You Are Not?

Describe in the space provided below how your interpersonal behaviors when you are depressed differ from your behaviors when you are not depressed. If you have been depressed for a long time, this may be difficult to do. Even so, you can probably identify periods when your depression was less severe than at other times. If that's the case, we encourage you to list the ways your interpersonal behavior when you're very depressed differs from your behavior when you're less depressed. An example of differences in interpersonal behaviors might be, *When I'm depressed, I keep to myself and don't speak unless somebody speaks to me first. When I'm not depressed (or I'm less depressed), I say hi when I see a neighbor or coworker.*

Having completed these exercises, what do you notice about how depressed people behave in their interactions with others and—more importantly—how *your* behavior differs when you are depressed? While it may not be pleasant to reflect on the ways you behave during periods of depression, especially the negative ways, take heart—identifying such behaviors is an important step in the process of changing them.

Another issue to consider is the types of behaviors you listed in the exercises. Did you describe verbal behaviors, nonverbal behaviors, or both? Perhaps you tend to think of your ways of interacting only in terms of your verbal behaviors (that is, what you say). As we will describe in the following sections, however, nonverbal behavior (that is, *how* you say what you say) is also a very important aspect of your interpersonal repertoire.

THE "WHAT" OF DEPRESSIVE COMMUNICATION

Before we get to nonverbal behaviors, let's first consider typical verbal communication of depressed people. In psychological lingo, we refer to this as the *content* of speech, meaning what people say. On a broad level, people tend to talk about negative themes when they are depressed. In this sense, the content of depressed people's speech is consistent with their mood. That is, depressed people feel blue, lethargic, uninterested in life, and hopeless, and they tend to talk about things that reflect those feelings. If you have spent time with people who are depressed, you may have noticed that they frequently bring up topics that are sad, discouraging, or otherwise unpleasant. For example, a depressed person may comment on how depressing the news is, emphasizing stories of crime, illness and death, economic woes, brutalities of war, and so on. In conversations, these downbeat themes often seem to take on lives of their own, spiraling further and further into negativity.

In addition to focusing on topics that are disheartening in their own right, people suffering from depression seem to have a knack for finding the negative in any situation, even one that may initially seem positive. Perhaps you have had the frustrating experience of describing something positive that has happened in your life, only to have another person disregard the positive and concentrate on the negative meanings of the event. The reverse scenario is that someone compliments you and you respond by explicitly or implicitly dismissing the compliment and bringing up negative features about yourself.

This tendency to highlight the negative can be considered a manifestation of the pessimism and hopelessness that characterize depression. Interestingly, depressed people are inclined to broach negative topics and emphasize the negative aspects of situations regardless of the subject of conversation; they are likely to make such comments about themselves, others, and impersonal objects or events.

Another communication pattern typical of depressed people involves *self-disclosure*, or revealing information about yourself that would not normally be known or discovered by others. An example would be sharing details about your performance on a recent exam, bringing up your personal relationship history, or revealing that you have a particular medical condition. Evidence suggests that depressed people self-disclose more than nondepressed people (Coyne 1976). What's more, this tends to happen even when the other person isn't asking for such information. In other words, depressed people often volunteer personal information about their feelings and experiences, and do so at inappropriate times. Given that depressed people tend to concentrate on the negative, it is likely that their self-disclosures will include talking about distress and unpleasant experiences.

Other research suggests that depressed people not only focus on the negative but also communicate more hostilely and aggressively in their close relationships (Segrin and Fitzpatrick 1992). That is, they are more apt to make disparaging remarks toward family members or to respond to requests with irritability and anger. Similarly, people who are depressed tend to make fewer constructive comments that resolve problems. These particular behaviors likely emerge as a result of the sadness, loss of pleasure, and fatigue that go along with depression.

These are some general examples of content-related communication behaviors typical of depressed people. Certainly, there are also more specific approaches to content that depressed people often take. These include self-handicapping, seeking negative feedback, and excessive reassurance seeking. We will discuss each of these in greater depth in chapters 5, 6, and 7.

EXERCISE 2.4: Experimenting with How You Say What You Say

We are going to ask you to become a scientist for a moment and to conduct a quick, simple experiment. Go to a mirror and stand in front of it. While looking at yourself, make the following statement: "I feel fine today." Next, repeat that same statement while smiling broadly and slightly raising your eyebrows. Finally, repeat the same statement while grimacing, furrowing your brow, and squinting slightly. What do you notice?

Besides feeling somewhat silly, you probably noticed that your message came across very differently each time you said it, even though the content (what you said) was exactly the same. This little experiment provides a basis for the distinction between content and process.

Now, let's turn to the issue of *how* people who are depressed tend to communicate.

THE "HOW" OF DEPRESSIVE COMMUNICATION

The notion of content is relatively easy to understand, primarily because most people routinely and intentionally pay attention to what others say. The concept of process, while also easy to understand, is probably less familiar. At times you may pay particular attention to the nonverbal behaviors of others, but more often you probably don't notice their nonverbal behaviors at a conscious level. That is, you could describe others' nonverbal behaviors in a given interpersonal setting if asked to do so, but you would not necessarily think about those behaviors otherwise.

Process refers to the "how" of communication. Process includes things such as tone, rate, pitch, and volume of speech; posture; facial expression; degree of eye contact; and physical proximity. You probably don't often actively notice such nonverbal behaviors, unless they are very different from what is viewed as normal in a given society or culture. It is precisely at this point that depression becomes relevant, because depressed people tend to communicate in ways that do indeed deviate from the norm.

Extensive research documents differences in nonverbal communication between depressed and nondepressed people, particularly with regard to the quality of speech. One of the most consistent findings in this area is that depressed people pause longer and more often while speaking. As a result, their speech is not fluent, but is broken up with lengthy periods of silence. Likewise, people who are depressed tend to talk less, speak more quietly, and speak more slowly than nondepressed people. Their speech varies less in pitch and tone, regardless of the subject matter, which lends a monotonous quality to their speech (Segrin 2000).

Depressed people also tend to have less variation in facial expression. Facial expressions of depressed people are often perceived as sad or flat, lacking emotional expression. More exacting research has found that depressed people are more likely to display a furrowed brow, down-turned mouth, and squinting eyes (Ganchrow et al. 1978). In addition, depressed people tend to make less eye contact while speaking and spend more time gazing downward. Similarly, depressed people often carry themselves with their head down. Depressed people also use relatively few nonverbal communicative behaviors such as gesturing with their hands and nodding their head. In contrast, they engage in more self-directed body contact, such as touching their face or rubbing or scratching their head, arms, or other body parts while interacting with others. Such self-directed body contact is often perceived as indicating social anxiety or discomfort.

EXERCISE 2.5: Self-Assessment of Depressive Interpersonal Behaviors

In this exercise, we list several interpersonal behaviors commonly seen among depressed people. We encourage you to read through the list and check off the behaviors that you recognize in yourself. This list is certainly not exhaustive, and it is important to note that not all of these behaviors are unique to depression; for example, some are also seen when people are anxious. Nonetheless, this exercise will help you identify areas of content and process that might be affected by your experience of depression.

Content

☐ Frequently bring up topics with a negative theme

☐ Focus on the negative aspects of topics when talking with others

☐ Dismiss compliments or praise from others

☐ Make disparaging comments about yourself or those close to you

☐ Frequently talk about your negative feelings, even if others don't ask about your feelings

☐ Frequently request assurances from those close to you

☐ Communicate critically, hostilely, or aggressively with those close to you

Process

☐   Speak infrequently or only after others speak to you

☐   Pause frequently and lengthily when speaking

☐   Speak quietly, such that others may have difficulty hearing you

☐   Speak in a monotonous tone

☐   Avoid eye contact with others

☐   Frequently hold head downward, looking toward the ground

☐   Routinely touch your face or other body parts while speaking with others

☐   Furrow brow, frown, or fail to smile when interacting with others

If you checked a number of the behaviors listed in this exercise, don't become too discouraged. The good news is that many of these depressive ways of communicating—particularly the process behaviors—tend to disappear as depressive symptoms improve. As you begin to feel better, your nonverbal communication patterns will become more like those of nondepressed people.

Our discussion thus far has focused on the "what" and the "how" of communication among depressed people, and exercise 2.5 helped you identify your own patterns. Nevertheless, we realize that it may be difficult to see how these behaviors show up in your daily experiences. To make the ideas in this chapter more relevant to your experiences, let's take a look at Steven, a former patient of ours who was depressed, and consider how these interpersonal behaviors reflected his depression.

■ Steven

Steven sat in our clinic waiting room wearing headphones, hunched over in a chair near the corner of the room. At first glance, it wasn't clear whether he was awake; his face was pointed directly at the floor, and his hair fell just long enough to hide his eyes. His hands were folded together on his lap. He happened to be the only person in the waiting room at that moment, so there was no doubt that he was the young man who had the appointment that afternoon, but he didn't respond right away to his name being called—twice.

Finally, his shoulders rose, his head lifted, and his fingers quickly fumbled to turn off his CD player. His gaze lifted halfway, then shifted back down to the floor.

"Steven?" He answered this time, but his words were too soft to be heard. As introductions were made, Steven briefly lifted his eyes to make eye contact, then rapidly dropped his head and focused on the floor. As we made our way back to the therapy room, Steven remained silent and kept his head down.

Once inside the room, he resumed his hunched position in a nearby chair. Steven slowly—and with much prompting—opened up and explained what led him to seek treatment at our clinic. He described persistent feelings of lethargy, boredom, and most painful of all, social isolation. When directly questioned, he said that he experienced sadness and bouts of crying, as well as fleeting thoughts that he would be "better off dead." He described his one previous romantic relationship and the pain he had experienced since it ended one year before. He reported that he had little contact with others outside of his immediate family. Moreover, he said that his relationships with immediate family members were strained because of his irritability toward them and frequent episodes of "snapping" and yelling at them. Steven's disparaging comments about himself made his sense of worthlessness almost tangible.

Steven spoke slowly, and occasionally he would stop in midsentence, as if he could not find the words to complete the thought he had started. At times it was difficult to resist the urge to finish his sentences for him. He made very infrequent eye contact, and it was fleeting the few times it occurred. His face revealed no emotions, except for brief moments when he appeared to fight back tears.

Analysis

Let's briefly revisit chapter 1 and examine the symptoms of depression that Steven showed. He clearly had a depressed mood, primarily when he felt lonely—which was most of the time. His "boredom" actually represented loss of ability to experience pleasure, even from activities that he had formerly enjoyed. In addition to having the two primary symptoms of major depression, he had a loss of energy, feelings of worthlessness, and thoughts of death. He also had difficulty concentrating, which likely played a role in the lengthy pauses when he spoke. Thus, Steven showed six of the nine criteria symptoms for major depressive disorder, and he was diagnosed accordingly.

Now, let's examine Steven's interpersonal behaviors more closely. A comparison of Steven's behaviors with the list in exercise 2.5 reveals that he showed both verbal and nonverbal ways of communicating common to depressed people. First, the content of his speech centered on the pain he experienced from the loss of a previous romantic relationship. This was to be expected, given that he had come to talk with a therapist. However, he also frequently criticized himself and made harsh, angry statements about members of his family. Second, the process, or nonverbal aspect, of Steven's communication was marked by a reluctance to speak and lack of emotional expression. His approach to communicating (for example, lack of eye contact, head down, soft speech) suggested that he was not interested in interacting with others, although that was far from the truth.

Steven demonstrated more nonverbal than verbal depressive behaviors, which is fairly common among those with severe levels of depression. However, it is important to emphasize two points here. First, depressed people differ greatly in their specific verbal and nonverbal behaviors. For example, some may show many of the content behaviors but not the withdrawn, quiet, slow speech patterns we saw in Steven. Second, the specific behaviors demonstrated by a depressed person can vary dramatically depending on the setting. Steven's quiet, withdrawn behaviors at the clinic contrasted with his irritable and hostile interactions with his family at home. Interestingly, this pattern of being overly reserved or acquiescing with strangers but extremely negative and antagonistic toward close relatives or romantic partners is quite common among people who are depressed.

THE "WITH WHOM" OF DEPRESSIVE COMMUNICATION

Now that we have described what sorts of things depressed people commonly discuss in social situations, as well as how they communicate through nonverbal behaviors, let's shift to the topic of *with whom* depressed people interact. Many of the behaviors that express anger or hostility occur in the context of close relationships, while the behaviors that express withdrawal tend to occur with strangers. So, with whom do depressed people interact and develop close relationships?

Research suggests that depressed people, or even people who are prone to become depressed, are more likely to choose relationship partners who contribute to the stress in their lives (Hammen 1999). Take a moment to remember exercise 1.4, when we asked you to list the most important people in your life, both positive and negative, and for each, describe what you get out of the relationship. When we ask our patients to do this exercise, it is not uncommon for them to say something like, "No wonder I'm depressed—look at the people I get into romantic relationships with." Relationships are rarely imposed upon people; rather, by and large, people seek out or drift toward certain types of partners, which is why patterns emerge in this exercise.

Consider, for example, a woman who for whatever reason tends to choose wrong when it comes to romantic partners, gravitating toward men who are unsupportive, preoccupied with themselves, and at times verbally abusive. It is no mystery that she is in for some stressful experiences, partly because of her choice. In this sense, her relationship choice can actually generate stress in her life.

Research supports the notion that depression-prone people tend to gravitate toward partners who themselves are prone to problems such as substance abuse, aggression, or depression (Hammen 1999). The end result is that both people in the relationship are likely to experience the stress of their own difficulties combined with the stress of their partner's problems—a stressful scenario indeed. If both experience depression, and both generate stress as a result of depression, stress and depression will abound for this couple. Patterns of partner selection may represent one way that depressed people contribute to their own experience of stress. If this rings true for you, then you might consider paying extra attention to the qualities of people you meet and question whether becoming involved with a given person as a friend or a romantic partner is likely to lead to undue stress.

We want to be very clear about some potential areas for misunderstanding. First, we are in no way stating that spouses or romantic partners of depressed people are bad partners. In fact, many relationship partners of depressed people are devoted and affectionate and want to help their mates traverse the difficult terrain of depression. Moreover, attempts to blame others for depressive experiences accomplish very little and should be avoided. Second, let us be clear that there is no reason to blame yourself about your pattern of mate selection. The pattern is what it is, and the question is simply whether you would like to change the pattern.

CHALLENGE: EXAMINE YOUR VERBAL AND NONVERBAL COMMUNICATION

Now that you understand how depression affects the content and process of your interpersonal interactions, we challenge you to begin the path to more effective communication.

EXERCISE 2.6:   Examining the Content and Process of Your Communication

Make at least seven photocopies of the Content and Process worksheet, and every day for the next week, use the form to carefully monitor the content of your speech and your nonverbal behaviors. Here are a few suggestions for using the form.

1.   Select a specific, time-limited interaction, such as one conversation you had with a coworker during the day. Record the date of the interaction, so that you will later be able to review the form as a way to measure your progress.

2.   Briefly describe the situation in the space provided, noting where and with whom it occurred. This section should be brief, focusing only on what you did in that interaction, not on what you were thinking or feeling, or what the other person did.

3.   After describing the event, rate the content of your conversation on the scales provided from 1 to 10. Was the general topic negative or positive? For example, conversations about health problems or traffic problems would receive negative ratings, whereas conversations about the good weather or your favorite team winning a big game would receive positive ratings.

4.   Rate the extent to which you highlighted the negative in the conversation. To continue the example of the good weather discussion, a statement such as "Now I'll

have to cut the grass again" emphasizes the negative. Also rate the extent to which you highlighted the positive in the conversation. An example of emphasizing the positive in this same situation would be "I'll be able to do some things outside that I've been wanting to do." It is important to rate positive and negative content separately, because they are not necessarily on the same continuum. That is, it's possible to make comments that highlight both the positive and negative aspects of a situation, as well as to emphasize neither positive nor negative aspects.

5. Another dimension to rate is the extent to which you dismissed the positive statements made by the other person. For example, in response to your coworker's assertion that it's a beautiful day, a statement such as "Yes, but it will probably rain tomorrow" clearly dismisses the positive. Other behaviors to rate include the extent to which you made critical or disparaging remarks about yourself or others, the extent to which you disclosed personal information (as well as the degree to which the disclosure was about negative or positive experiences), and the degree to which you asked the other person to reassure you or comfort you.

6. While this worksheet captures most aspects of conversational content, there may be some features that are unique to a particular exchange. Feel free to use the "Other" blank at the bottom of the form to include and rate these behaviors.

7. Finally, add your responses to arrive at a total score that can range from 10 to 100. Higher scores represent the expression of more negative content. As you complete several worksheets over the course of the week, pay attention not only to changes in your total scores but also to particular areas (for example, dismissing the positive) or interaction partners (for example, your spouse) that are consistently associated with higher negative scores.

After you have completed the content portion of the form, go on to complete the process section.

1. Rate the extent to which you initiated the interaction. For example, if your spouse or roommate is in the kitchen and you go from your bedroom to the kitchen and start a conversation, you would rate that as a 10. In contrast, if your spouse or roommate comes from the kitchen to your bedroom and starts a conversation, you would rate that much lower.

2. Rate your facial expression during the interaction, paying particular attention to how much you furrowed your brow and how much you smiled.

3. Rate the qualities of your speech, including the volume, variation in tone, and frequency of pauses while speaking.

4. Finally, rate behaviors such as frequency of eye contact, good posture (for example, head up, shoulders up), and the extent to which you touched your face or body or fidgeted with your hands while speaking.

Some process behaviors, like facial expression, may initially be difficult to judge yourself, so you may consider asking someone close to you to help in rating them. Remember, however, that the goal is for you to learn to identify these behaviors in yourself as they happen and then modify them. It is important not to rely too much on others to help you with the form.

You can rate other relevant process characteristics at the bottom of the worksheet. Then, add up your responses to arrive at a total score ranging from 10 to 100. Once again, higher scores reflect more negative process characteristics. As you complete these worksheets, notice particular dimensions (for example, eye contact) and settings in which you achieve higher scores.

Worksheet: Content and Process

Date: _____

Briefly describe the situation, including with whom you interacted: _____

_____

_____

_____

Content

General topic	negative	1	2	3	4	5	6	7	8	9	10	positive
Highlighted negative	more	1	2	3	4	5	6	7	8	9	10	less
Highlighted positive	less	1	2	3	4	5	6	7	8	9	10	more
Dismissed others' positive remarks	more	1	2	3	4	5	6	7	8	9	10	less
Critical remarks												
Toward self	more	1	2	3	4	5	6	7	8	9	10	less
Toward others	more	1	2	3	4	5	6	7	8	9	10	less
Self-disclosure												
Intensity	more	1	2	3	4	5	6	7	8	9	10	less
Topic	negative	1	2	3	4	5	6	7	8	9	10	positive
Asked for assurance	more	1	2	3	4	5	6	7	8	9	10	less

Other: _____

Total score (10–100): _____

Worksheet: Content and Process (continued)

Process

		1	2	3	4	5	6	7	8	9	10	
Initiated interaction	less	1	2	3	4	5	6	7	8	9	10	more
Facial expression												
Furrowed brow	more	1	2	3	4	5	6	7	8	9	10	less
Smiled	less	1	2	3	4	5	6	7	8	9	10	more
Speech qualities												
Volume	quiet	1	2	3	4	5	6	7	8	9	10	clear
Tone	monotonous	1	2	3	4	5	6	7	8	9	10	varied
Pauses	more	1	2	3	4	5	6	7	8	9	10	less
Eye contact	less	1	2	3	4	5	6	7	8	9	10	more
Good posture	less	1	2	3	4	5	6	7	8	9	10	more
Touched or rubbed face or body	more	1	2	3	4	5	6	7	8	9	10	less
Other:		1	2	3	4	5	6	7	8	9	10	

Total score (10–100): _____

3 Depression and Social Skills: The Real Story

In this chapter, we build upon the connection between communication style and depression presented in chapter 2. We indirectly addressed social skills in chapter 2 by describing some common verbal and nonverbal communicative behaviors of depressed people, and then we encouraged you to systematically observe and identify your own behavior patterns in interpersonal settings. We hope that the final exercise in chapter 2 helped you identify aspects of the content and process of your communication that hinder your interpersonal relations. In this chapter, we provide a broader overview of social skills among people with depression, focusing primarily on the content of communication.

DIFFERING PERSPECTIVES

The perceptions of social skills differ substantially between those who are talking and those who are listening. Stated another way, your view of your own behaviors in social settings may not agree with the way that other people experience your behaviors. For example, consider a woman who experiences anxiety over a presentation she must make at work. She has worried considerably prior to the presentation, and during the presentation, she has rapid heartbeat, mild trembling in her hands and legs, and sweating. Her voice cracks, and she mispronounces certain words that she would normally pronounce correctly. After the presentation, she reflects upon her performance and feels discouraged because she experienced those symptoms of anxiety. When she receives feedback from coworkers (including her boss), however, she is surprised to hear that none of them appeared to have noticed any of her symptoms of anxiety. What's more, they congratulate her on making a great presentation. Clearly, her perception of her presentation is quite different from other people's perception. This type of scenario is actually rather common among depressed and nondepressed people alike.

Depressing Self-Perceptions

You can probably relate to the experience of viewing your own performance in presentations as worse than observers rate your performance. But what about broader, more generalized views of social behaviors, interacting with others in general, not just when speaking in front of groups? Everybody has beliefs about their social skills, meaning their ability to effectively interact and communicate with others.

EXERCISE 3.1:   What Are Your Social Skills?

In the space provided, list some perceptions you hold about your own social skills (for example, *I am competent, I'm a smooth talker, I stumble over words, My comments sound dumb,* or *I make a good first impression*).

_____

_____

_____

_____

Pay attention to the ways in which you described your social skills. While most people will list both positive and negative features (especially positive), people who are depressed often hold extraordinarily negative impressions of their social competence. This is true with regard to both specific situations and social functioning in general. This is not terribly surprising, given that depressed people tend to hold negative views of many things, especially their own characteristics. Nevertheless, the unfavorable self-evaluation of social skills among depressed people appears to go beyond low self-esteem. Following are some examples of the types of beliefs depressed and nondepressed people tend to hold about their capabilities in social settings.

Depressed People	Nondepressed People
I am unable to effectively initiate conversations.	I feel comfortable talking with most people.
I can't think of things to say when I interact with others.	I stand up for myself when it is called for.
I worry that I will say the wrong thing.	I effectively get my point across to others.
I let people walk all over me.	I am able to approach people and start conversations.
People think I am boring.	Others are interested in what I have to say.

As you can see, depressed and nondepressed people tend to hold quite different perceptions of their own social skills. Interestingly, some research indicates that depressed people may be more accurate judges of their social skills (Lewinsohn et al. 1980). In other words, nondepressed people often overestimate their interpersonal ability and competence. Depressed people, in contrast, are likely to underestimate their abilities, but to a lesser degree. Apparently, it can be beneficial to overestimate your abilities, as long as you don't go overboard. We're not endorsing self-aggrandizement. Indeed, people who grossly overestimate their interpersonal abilities experience a unique set of problems. However, it appears that if you are going to err in the assessment of your own social skills, doing so in the positive direction may be more psychologically healthy.

Others' Views of Depressed People

Depressed people tend to hold negative views of their social abilities, while nondepressed people tend to overestimate their social skills somewhat. Given these patterns of self-evaluation, how do nondepressed people view the social skills of those who are depressed? Evidence is less consistent, but a general trend suggests that observers and conversational partners of depressed people rate their social skills somewhat lower than those of nondepressed people (Segrin 1990). So, consistent with the self-views of depressed people, nondepressed observers also tend to hold more negative views of depressed people's social skills. However, their views are not as negative as the self-view held by depressed people. Put another way, people perceive shortcomings in depressed people's social skills but do not view them as being as socially inept as depressed people often view themselves.

WHAT'S THE REAL STORY? RESEARCH ON SOCIAL SKILLS AND DEPRESSION

The story thus far can be summed up as follows: depressed people view themselves as extremely socially inept; nondepressed people view themselves (inaccurately, at times) as extremely socially competent; and nondepressed people view depressed people as less socially adept than others, but they do not view depressed people as negatively as depressed people view themselves.

All of that is interesting, and worth knowing, but it is still at the level of perceptions. What does research say about the actual social skills of depressed people?

As we discussed in chapter 2, depressed people do indeed have nonverbal communication habits (for example, poor speech quality and lack of eye contact) that suggest problems with social skills. And as we'll discuss in chapter 4, depressed people tend to be less assertive in social settings and consequently are less likely to get what they want from interpersonal interactions. Likewise, the tendency of depressed people to raise negative topics and to disclose negative feelings at inappropriate times may be considered deficits in social skills. Not surprisingly, such behaviors are associated with greater rejection by others.

Overall, it appears that depressed people do indeed have some trouble with social skills, although the problems are most likely not as great as they may believe. Moreover, people who interact with depressed people are likely to view them as less socially competent than others, although it is important to note again that their views of depressed people are usually not as harsh as depressed people's self-evaluations. Thus, depressed people are not completely socially deficient, as they may think. However, there are certain areas in which their behavior is likely to be problematic.

These problems manifest in two forms. First, there is a general withdrawal of positive social behaviors. This is evidenced by poor eye contact, failure to smile, fewer assertive behaviors, and less speech in general. Second, when communication does occur, it appears to be largely negative in both process and content. This is seen in nonverbal behaviors like furrowing of the brow and verbal behaviors like discussing primarily negative topics, including negative self-disclosure.

■ Raquel

Raquel was a woman in her early forties who came to our clinic because she was concerned that she was depressed. Like many people who suffer from depression, she also experienced a fair amount of anxiety, especially in social settings. Evaluation revealed that Raquel met diagnostic criteria for major depression and dysthymia; she had double depression. In spite of her experiences of anxiety, she did not meet diagnostic criteria for any particular anxiety disorder. Raquel had been divorced for seven years before seeking treatment, after her relationship with her husband slowly deteriorated due to his heavy use of alcohol. Her husband had been verbally abusive regularly, too, and at times he became physically abusive toward her after several drinks. At the time she came to see us, Raquel lived with her two teenage daughters, both of whom were becoming increasingly difficult to manage and at times became aggressive toward her.

Raquel reported chronic symptoms of depression that first developed during her marriage. She was generally able to hold a job and provide for herself and her daughters, although her symptoms occasionally worsened to the point that they interfered with her productivity at work. In addition to depressive symptoms, Raquel described feeling lonely and said that she strongly desired to have a friend, someone to talk to and confide in. She especially wanted a romantic partner, but she said she would be happy for the time being to just have someone to talk with, go to an occasional movie with, and so on.

Raquel told us that she had always been somewhat shy and did not feel comfortable approaching people or starting conversations. She also felt as though she couldn't think of anything to say when interacting with others or that her statements sounded dumb to her after she made them. This feeling of social awkwardness was particularly troubling to her, because she longed for close relationships but believed that others did not want to be around her.

Raquel also reported problems asserting her desires and interests. For fear of rejection from others, she refrained from telling people when she didn't like something. As a result, she was often stuck covering for people on the night shift at work and giving in to her daughters' demands for increasing freedom. At others times, however, she would become extremely frustrated and explode—yelling at others and aggressively voicing her opinions and indignation at feeling slighted.

Over the years, Raquel had observed that her social skills were at their worst during times when she felt more depressed (that is, during major depressive episodes). This observation set up a cycle: she would notice an increase in depressive symptoms, then expect to perform worse in social settings, which in turn led to even more depression, and so on.

Analysis

Like many depressed people, Raquel experienced anxiety and other difficulties in social situations. As is common, some of her problematic social behaviors preceded her depression, but others developed after or were exacerbated by her experiences of depression. Raquel clearly had trouble asserting herself in social settings, which resulted in problems in a variety of settings, including work and home. Her social reticence made her feel even lonelier. Moreover, Raquel's belief that she was socially awkward led her to doubt her social abilities and to further avoid interacting with others. Were her beliefs correct?

Consistent with research on the social skills of depressed people in general, the answer is yes and no. It's true that Raquel was sometimes ineffective at fully expressing herself when she spoke. For example, she would often hint at things she desired or disliked, rather than asking others directly. As a result, others frequently did not recognize her statements as veiled requests, as she hoped they would. In addition, Raquel's statements did come across as somewhat awkward when she was especially anxious. Nevertheless, it would be unfair and inaccurate to say that Raquel's social deficits were as great and pervasive as she believed them to be.

Treatment with Raquel focused on resolving her symptoms of depression, as well as helping her to develop more functional social skills. Treatment also worked to assist Raquel in more accurately evaluating her social competence. Thanks to Raquel's willingness to practice and take interpersonal risks, her depressive symptoms improved, and she became more assertive and more willing to interact with others. She no longer responded to others with an outpouring of frustration and anger. She was successful in saying no to covering for others on the graveyard shift at work, although she continued to have some difficulties setting limits for her daughters.

CHALLENGE: EVALUATE YOUR SOCIAL SKILLS

Just as Raquel worked to develop a more realistic perception of her social abilities, we encourage you to again adopt the role of a scientist conducting experiments. Whether or not you feel that you have difficulties in interpersonal settings, we challenge you to conduct social "experiments" and test hypotheses about your social skills.

EXERCISE 3.2:   What Are Your Beliefs about Your Social Skills?

Use the Social Experiment worksheet to test your hypotheses, or beliefs, about your social skills. Make four or five copies of the blank Social Experiment worksheet so that you can test your social skills in several settings. First, take a look at the sample Social Experiment worksheet. Then read the instructions below. Then fill out your own worksheet.

1. Choose a situation and briefly describe what you did and what the other person or people did. Pick a situation that has a beginning, middle, and end. Avoid making interpretations about what happened or describing your thoughts or emotions at this point. Simply describe what happened, where, and when, as if you were watching the situation unfold on a movie screen.

2. In the next column, list the hypotheses, or beliefs, you hold about your social capabilities in that situation. Note that you probably hold several beliefs about your social skills (for example, *I can't start a conversation*, *I sound awkward when I talk*, and *Others find me interesting*). We encourage you to list each belief about your social skills in that specific situation and then examine the evidence for and against each. If you have enough space, you can list several hypotheses on the same form.

3. Next, describe specific evidence from the situation that supports your hypothesis. This would be any behavior or response that suggests that your beliefs accurately reflect your social performance in that situation.

4. List specific evidence from the situation that contradicts your hypothesis. This would be behaviors or responses that are inconsistent with your stated hypothesis.

5. Finally, indicate in the last column whether your hypothesis was supported or unsupported by the evidence. It may be difficult to say with certainty that a hypothesis was entirely supported or entirely unsupported, so we suggest that you rate the extent to which your hypothesis was supported on a scale from 1 to 10, where 1 means completely unsupported and 10 means completely supported.

Complete worksheets about situations in several settings (for example, at home, at work, out shopping, at school) and test whether the beliefs you hold about your social skills mirror reality. If you are depressed, you are likely overemphasizing the negative. To counter this, make an extra effort to consider the positive responses from others. Also, examine whether there are specific areas in which your social skills could stand improvement. For example, when you feel uncomfortable in a social setting, do you abruptly end the conversation and leave? Are there specific settings in which you are more likely to have trouble with interpersonal skills?

If you recognize a pattern of being unassertive—particularly if you have problems coming up with situations in which to test your beliefs about your social skills because you avoid interacting with others—then you'll find it especially helpful to read chapter 4, where we discuss in greater depth the negative consequences of interpersonal inhibition, as well as how to overcome it. Later chapters will guide you in improving other aspects of your communication and interaction. You may also want to consider investing in a self-help book for developing social skills or seeing a therapist or counselor who has experience in social skills training.

Worksheet: Social Experiment

Situation	Hypothesis about Social Skills	Evidence for Hypothesis	Evidence against Hypothesis	Hypothesis Supported? (1 to 10)

Worksheet: Social Experiment

Situation	Hypothesis about Social Skills	Evidence for Hypothesis	Evidence against Hypothesis	Hypothesis Supported? (1 to 10)
During a break at work, a coworker sat down beside me to have a cup of coffee. I said, "Hi," and she responded, "Hi, how are you?" I told her that I was fine but busy trying to complete a project before the deadline. She asked about the project, and I described it to her. Then she said that she needed to get back to work, and she left.	She finds me boring.	■ She left the room after I described the project.	■ She sat down beside me. ■ She asked me how I was and about my project. ■ She listened to me. ■ She smiled at me. ■ She left because she had to return to work.	2

4 Engaging with Your Social Environment

Up to this point, we have examined the content and process of how you interact with others when you are depressed, and we have examined how depression affects your social skills—and your perception of your social skills. We hope that you have accepted the challenges at the end of chapters 2 and 3 and that you are now actively collecting and examining data about your behaviors in interpersonal situations. Although reading this book will help you to develop a better understanding of how your interpersonal behaviors are linked to your depression, it is by doing the exercises that you will bring about significant changes in your depression.

As we have emphasized, one common feature of depression is general social withdrawal. In fact, even if you consider yourself to be an outgoing person, you have probably experienced firsthand the dampening effect that depression can have on your social endeavors. You may have noticed that you no longer desire the same level of social activity as in previous times or that you feel more irritable or less patient when interacting with others. You may even just want to stay by yourself and avoid the hassles of interacting with other people. Don't lose heart. As discouraging as those feelings can be, they are all common characteristics of depression that can be thwarted by actively following the exercises presented in this book.

In this chapter, we will explore in depth the social withdrawal and social inhibition that often accompany depression. In particular, we will highlight one feature of interpersonal inhibition that may be keeping you from getting the most out of your relationships and from breaking the cycle of depression: avoidance of interpersonal conflict. We will conclude this chapter with a challenge that will help you overcome your interpersonal inhibitions and break free of depression.

INTERPERSONAL INHIBITION AND DEPRESSION

Interpersonal inhibition may be the end point of a number of different paths. Perhaps you have felt shy and avoided the spotlight for as long as you can remember. Or perhaps you had less energy and enthusiasm than usual when you were in the initial stages of depression, and so you stopped making the effort to develop and maintain relationships the way you did in the past. Or perhaps you had some negative, hurtful experiences with others and decided that it wasn't worth the risk to make yourself vulnerable to those experiences again. Exercise 4.1 will help you understand when and how your patterns of social avoidance developed.

EXERCISE 4.1: Exploring the Origins of Your Social Avoidance

Were you generally shy during childhood or adolescence? If so, in what ways does your avoidance in social settings now mirror your shyness as a youngster?

_____

_____

_____

Looking back to the beginning stages of your current episode of depression, in what ways did your social activities and efforts to initiate social contact change from when you weren't depressed? What interpersonal behaviors did you stop doing at that time, and what interpersonal behaviors did you start doing?

_____

_____

_____

What experiences in your past may have played a role in the development of social avoidance? Can you think of times when being assertive or speaking out in social situations backfired on you and you got hurt or embarrassed?

_____

_____

_____

Depression: The Opposite of Participation?

Regardless of how it began, avoidance in social situations has a way of weaving itself through the fabric of your life when you are depressed. Daniel Boroto (1999, personal communication) suggested that avoidance, or inhibition, captures the true essence of depression. He argued that depression, at its root, is simply the opposite of participation. While this is a broad and simplistic way of thinking about depression, it highlights the idea that depression can drain your resources to the point that you become more a passive recipient of life than an active participant in life. As a result, you may begin to not only accept life's occurrences without pushing for what you want but also avoid behaviors or situations that have the potential to be unpleasant.

But isn't that something that everyone does, regardless of whether they are depressed or not? Isn't avoiding unpleasant situations a natural way to maximize your enjoyment and minimize your distress? To a certain extent, that is true. But consider the differences between Joe and Sharon, whom we describe below.

■ Joe

Joe doesn't attend parties and get-togethers at his friend Roxanne's house because he is highly allergic to Roxanne's two Siamese cats, Lester and Chester. Like most behaviors, Joe's avoidance has both positive and negative consequences. Joe's avoidance is positive in that it promotes his physical well-being and spares him the discomfort associated with a severe allergic reaction. The negative consequences, on the other hand, are a possible reduction in social activities and missing out on the good times to be had at Roxanne's get-togethers. Fortunately for Joe, he has several other good friends and can do other enjoyable things when Roxanne has a party, so his avoidance of Roxanne's get-togethers doesn't lead him to feel upset or lonely. Hence, in this particular scenario, Joe's avoidance leads to more positive than negative outcomes.

◼ Sharon

Sharon, like Joe, doesn't attend Roxanne's parties because she is allergic to Lester and Chester. Thus, she too experiences the positive consequence of not having an allergic reaction. Sharon differs from Joe, however, in that she has a much smaller circle of friends than he does. In fact, Roxanne is her primary source of companionship, and outside of their relationship, Sharon feels quite cut off from the rest of the world. When Roxanne hosts get-togethers, Sharon typically stays at home feeling lonely and sad.

That alone makes Sharon's avoidance more negative than positive, but there is more to it than that. Sharon doesn't just avoid Roxanne's get-togethers, she also avoids many other situations that have the potential for unpleasant experiences. For example, she also skips holiday parties at work because one of her coworkers routinely has one drink too many and says things that make Sharon feel uncomfortable. Likewise, she avoids asking her boss for a raise because she doesn't want to be pushy, and she avoids giving her opinions during meetings because she doesn't want people to think she is stupid. While each of these instances of avoidance may be minor in and of itself, their combination leads to a lifestyle of interpersonal avoidance.

Analysis

The cases of Joe and Sharon are simply fictional examples of avoidance, yet in certain ways, they illustrate the outcomes of avoidance among nondepressed and depressed people. That is, all people avoid things. The nature and consequences of the avoidance, however, tend to differ when you are depressed. For one thing, as we saw in Sharon's case, depression is often associated with smaller social networks. The result of this is a magnification of the negative effects of avoidance. As you can easily imagine, larger social networks afford you more opportunities for positive interpersonal experiences. When your social network is already limited, however, difficulties or disturbances in any given relationship have a larger impact on your well-being.

But more importantly, the negative consequences of social avoidance are also due to the way depressed people engage in avoidance. Later in this chapter, we discuss interpersonal conflict avoidance, which is arguably the most pernicious form of avoidance. First, though, take a minute to do exercise 4.2 and list some of the negative and positive consequences of social avoidance in your life.

EXERCISE 4.2:   The Benefits and Costs of Social Avoidance

In the chart below, list some ways that you engage in social avoidance, and then describe both positive and negative consequences of that avoidance. We provide one example to help you get started.

Social Avoidance	Positive Consequences	Negative Consequences
My coworker Javier tries to take the work assignment I wanted. I say nothing.	■ Avoided an argument with Javier. ■ I didn't look pushy or entitled in front of my coworkers. ■ Avoided potential embarrassment of making a scene and still not getting the assignment.	■ I got stuck with an assignment I didn't want. ■ My opportunity for advancement at work is less with this assignment. ■ I felt angry the rest of the day.

AVOIDANCE IN DEPRESSED PEOPLE

We have discussed the connection between depression and social avoidance, how your social avoidance may have developed, and some of the consequences of general social avoidance. Now let's examine the manifestations of social avoidance in depression. That is, what does social avoidance look like among depressed people?

Low Assertiveness

One of the most common forms of social avoidance in the context of depression is low assertiveness. Research supports the notion that people who are depressed are more likely to be unassertive (Youngren and Lewinsohn 1980). What's more, people who are unassertive are also more likely to become depressed in the future (Ball et al. 1994). So what is assertiveness, and why is it so important to your depression?

Assertion has been defined as "expressing thoughts, feelings, and beliefs in direct, honest, and appropriate ways which respect the rights of other people" (Lange and Jakubowksi 1976, 38). Thus, when people are low in assertiveness, or unassertive, they hold back and conceal their thoughts, feelings, or beliefs.

DISTINGUISHING ASSERTION FROM AGGRESSION

A common misperception is that being assertive in social interactions is the same as being aggressive. In reality, however, there are some key distinctions between assertion and aggression. First, notice that the definition of assertion ends with "appropriate ways which respect the rights of other people." Assertion involves expressing your views while still respecting others. In contrast, *aggression* has been defined as "self-expression which is characterized by violating others' rights and demeaning others in an attempt to achieve one's own objectives" (Lange and Jakubowksi 1976, 38–39).

In the following scenarios, we list some examples of how assertive, aggressive, and passive behaviors differ.

Scenario: You are at a department store to purchase a last-minute gift on your way to a birthday party. You are standing at the front of the line, but the cashier is ignoring you while obviously carrying on a personal conversation on the telephone. What do you do?

Aggressive response: "Hey, can't you see that I'm standing here? Where do you get off talking with your girlfriend instead of doing your job?"

Assertive response: "Excuse me, I'm in a hurry. Please ring up my purchase."

Passive response: Wait without saying anything, or do something like clearing your throat to indirectly catch the attention of the cashier.

Scenario: You get off of work at 5:00 P.M., and you have a dinner reservation for 6:00. At 4:45, your boss comes to your office and tells you that she has an important project that she wants you to finish tonight. You know that it will take at least two hours to complete the job. What do you do?

Aggressive response: "Are you kidding me? It's already 4:45, and I have plans this evening. You can forget about it being done tonight."

Assertive response: "I already made plans for this evening, but I'll be glad to tackle this project first thing tomorrow morning."

Passive response: "Well, I had planned to go to dinner tonight, but I suppose I'll just have to do that some other time."

Scenario: You are at a coffee shop with an acquaintance, and the conversation shifts to politics. Your acquaintance expresses some political views with which you strongly disagree. What do you do?

Aggressive response: "You're wrong. How can you believe that garbage?"

Assertive response: "I disagree with you on that issue. I think . . ." (state your own views on the issue).

Passive response: Say nothing and nod your head.

As you can see in these examples, assertion and aggression (and also passivity) are distinct. Nevertheless, if you have difficulty being assertive, then it may feel as though you are being aggressive when you are in reality being assertive. For example, asking someone not to cut in front of you in line may be difficult to do, but it's not aggressive. Fortunately, this misperception can be changed with practice (we'll say more about this later).

Low assertiveness, in essence, is driven by the desire to avoid interpersonal conflict. Two aspects of assertive behavior may be very difficult for you when you are depressed. First, asserting yourself requires active engagement with others, which forces you to overcome feelings of general social anxiety, in addition to overcoming the lethargy and indifference that you may feel when you are depressed. Second, and more importantly, assertive behaviors require you to make explicit requests to others. It is at this point that the stage for potential disharmony is set, because requests prompt a response, be it positive or negative. Simply stated, the difficult thing about making requests is that people can say no. Thus, to reach this point, you must conquer general social anxiety and place yourself in a position that allows for the possibility of negative, rejecting responses from others. It is the possibility of rejection that is the sticking point for many people, especially depressed people. That is, people who are depressed overcome social inhibition and inertia, but they are often unwilling to knowingly make themselves vulnerable to interpersonal rejection.

Make no mistake, opening yourself up to rejection is tough. Further, it may be that past experiences of rejection have made you very leery of putting yourself in a position to be rejected again. In this sense, being unassertive at times can be a reasonable response, in the same way that Joe and Sharon's avoidance of the cats kept them from experiencing an allergic reaction. As in Sharon's case, however, unassertiveness can also lead to negative consequences, like a worsening of your depression. We will discuss this problem—and how to solve it—later in this chapter.

Shyness

A related example of social avoidance in the context of depression is shyness. Shyness, or tension and inhibition in social situations, is relatively common. Social psychologist Philip Zimbardo (1977) has conducted several general population surveys, finding that approximately 40 percent of the population currently classified themselves as shy and 80 percent reported being shy at some point in their life. Of course, not all shy people are depressed, and not all depressed people are shy. Nonetheless, there is considerable research supporting the notion that shy people are more vulnerable to depression (Cheek and Buss 1981, Joiner 1997).

THE IMPORTANT ROLE OF LONELINESS

Given that not all shy people become depressed, under what circumstances do shy people become depressed? In a study examining the interaction of shyness and social support as it relates to depressive symptoms, depression increased among shy people only in the absence of social support, and it occurred as a function of loneliness. That is, shy people with an adequate amount of social support (that is, shy people who were not lonely) did not show increases in depressive symptoms. Only those people who were both shy and lonely experienced a worsening of depression (Joiner 1997). Hence, shyness alone does not appear to be a vulnerability factor for depression. Among people who are lonely, however, those who are also shy are more likely to become depressed than their more outgoing counterparts.

One implication of that finding is that good social relations may serve as a protective factor against depression among shy people. That is, if you consider yourself to be shy, it is important for you to maintain an active and supportive social network. If you are unsatisfied with your social relations, however, you may be more likely to experience depression.

NOT MAKING WAVES: INTERPERSONAL CONFLICT AVOIDANCE

As we've said, general avoidance in social situations is quite common among people who are depressed. What's more, evidence suggests that depression is frequently preceded by anxiety of some form (Kovacs et al. 1989). Anxiety, of course, is characterized by avoidance of some feared object, thought, or event. While anxiety and general social avoidance certainly play a role in depression, a more specific form of social avoidance appears to play the lead role: avoidance of interpersonal conflict.

There is good reason to emphasize interpersonal conflict avoidance, as opposed to generalized avoidance, as a crucial component in your depression. As we discussed earlier, assertiveness is often quite difficult when you are depressed. Assertiveness is a necessary part of successful conflict negotiation. Conflict goes beyond mere interpersonal contact and often requires you to assume a confrontational position. Furthermore, assertive actions expose you to the possibility of a variety of negative responses from others, such as anger, hostility, and rejection. Avoiding assertive behaviors allows you to escape the discomfort of negative reactions from others. It also, however, lessens your chances of getting what you want from interactions.

How Interpersonal Conflict Avoidance Maintains Your Depression

If avoiding interpersonal conflicts maintains harmony, then how does it create and maintain depression? Although it may seem contradictory at first to think that maintaining harmony creates depression, two primary consequences of avoiding conflict make it more likely that you will become depressed and stay depressed. First, and probably most importantly, avoiding conflict in social settings brings about loss.

LOSS

The connection between submission and loss is fairly straightforward. By submitting to others and avoiding asserting yourself, you stand to lose in a number of ways. When you avoid conflict, you may lose status, material possessions, rights, and—potentially—your freedom. Consider a situation in which you are overcharged for a product but do not try to remedy the situation; you would stand to lose money. Or consider the scenario described earlier in which your boss asks you to work late. If you agree to do so, you stand to lose time and the pleasure of having dinner at a nice restaurant, at the least.

EXERCISE 4.3:   What Have You Lost by Avoiding Conflict?

In the spaces below, list specific things (for example, time, money, or dignity) that you have lost as a result of avoiding potential conflicts.

Potential conflict avoided:

Losses:

_____

_____

Potential conflict avoided:

_____

Losses:

_____

_____

Potential conflict avoided:

_____

Losses:

_____

_____

Potential conflict avoided:

_____

Losses:

_____

_____

We hope that the connection between your avoidance of interpersonal conflict and consequent losses is becoming more obvious. While conflict avoidance leads to loss, loss in turn is an important trigger of depression. Think back to chapter 1, when we discussed the causes of depression. Stressors, including losses, are a common cause of depression. Also, examine your answers to the question in exercise 1.4 about recent stressors in your life. How many of those involve some form of loss? Losses of jobs, loved ones, relationships, physical abilities, social status, and material possessions are all associated with the onset of depression.

DECREASED SOCIAL CONTACT

A second way that interpersonal conflict avoidance may create and maintain depression in your life is through a decrease of social contact. Social contacts provide *social reinforcement,* or positive interactions with others. Social reinforcement, in turn, is related to depression. Several researchers have persuasively argued that a lack of social reinforcement or social support is implicated in the onset of depression and acts to maintain, or lengthen, depression (Lara, Leader, and Klein 1997; Lewinsohn and Libet 1972; Rehm 1977).

In the context of depression as a lack of participation, it is easy to imagine how a lack of positive social interactions and social support structure maintains your depression. As you may have experienced yourself, being alone leaves no chance for positive encounters to pull your thoughts and feelings away from the suffering of depression.

Okay, so that's the bad news. The good news is that research evidence also indicates that the presence of social support actually speeds recovery from depression (McLeod, Kessler, and Landis 1992). That is, by becoming more active, more assertive, and less avoidant in social settings, you can help yourself recover from depression.

We realize that you may be a bit skeptical at this point. That's okay for now. The important thing is to give it a shot and then evaluate whether it helps you. From our experience—and more importantly, from solid research—we can verify that becoming more socially active and assertive does indeed help you leave the quagmire of depression in the past. Consider James's story.

◼ James

James was in his midtwenties when he first came to our clinic. Over the past few months, he had been having difficulties sleeping at night and "getting going" during the day. He sought treatment from his primary care physician, who screened him for symptoms of depression and recommended that he be evaluated further by a mental health professional.

James said that in addition to waking up very early in the morning and being unable to fall asleep again, he also had fatigue, loss of appetite, weight loss, difficulty concentrating, and sadness. When James was asked to list the most important people in his life and what he got out of the relationships (see exercise 1.4), his list was extremely short: it included only his immediate family. James hadn't misunderstood the question; his social network really was quite limited.

By this point, it seemed fairly clear that James was experiencing a major depressive episode. Given his limited social network, his interpersonal behaviors and relationships were likely connected to his depression. James described himself as shy in social settings. It wasn't that he didn't like people or didn't want to talk with others—in fact, he very much desired more relationships in his life. Rather, he felt anxious and awkward with other people. He explained that he didn't know what to say or how to start conversations, so he typically kept to himself. At times, he had something to say and wanted to say it, but then he pondered about *whether* he should say it until too much time had passed to actually say it.

James spent a lot of time by himself, but even when he was in a group (for example, at work), he still felt lonely. He also described himself as an angry person. Although this initially seemed at odds with his shy, meek presentation, he discussed in detail how outraged he became when others "disrespected" him. For example, he seethed with anger when people cut in front of him in line at the grocery store, when people at work made an appointment with him but didn't show up, and when a coworker routinely made fun of James's hometown as a "hick town." In spite of his anger, James remained silent. He often replayed these events in his mind and thought of what he would have done or said to "put them in their place."

It became clear that James's anger, sadness, and loneliness were all related to each other. In fact, by keeping track of how he behaved in his social interactions and how he felt afterward, James discovered that he became angry after situations in which he remained silent and that he felt most sad and depressed after he became angry. A primary goal of treatment, therefore, focused on helping James to become more assertive. It was difficult at first for James to realize that he had a right to stand up for himself and that asserting himself was not the same as being aggressive, but as he became more assertive, he noticed that he felt less angry and sad. Moreover, he noted that others actually began to show him more respect and that he began to enjoy interpersonal relationships more.

CHALLENGE: CONQUER YOUR INTERPERSONAL INHIBITION

In chapters 2 and 3, the challenges were designed to help you recognize your verbal and nonverbal behaviors in interpersonal settings and to examine some of your beliefs about your abilities in social settings. Now that you have identified what you do in social situations, the next step is to change your behaviors so as to attain the best possible outcomes, just as James did. For most people who are depressed—and some who aren't—this involves conquering interpersonal inhibitions, particularly in situations that have the potential for conflict. The following exercise is designed to help you do just that. If you feel that you need additional help in developing assertiveness beyond what we offer in this book, we suggest reading *The Assertiveness Workbook* by Randy Patterson (2000, New Harbinger Publications).

EXERCISE 4.4:   Overcoming Your Inhibition

Make several photocopies of the Overcoming Inhibitions worksheet. As with the challenges in chapters 2 and 3, start by selecting a specific, time-limited interaction, such as a conversation you had with an employee at a grocery store.

1. After you have selected an interaction, record the date that it occurred, so that you will later be able to review the forms as a way to measure your progress.

2. Next, briefly describe the situation in the space provided, noting where and with whom it occurred. This section should be brief, focusing only on what you did in that interaction, not on what you were thinking or feeling.

3. After describing the event, circle the score that best reflects your behaviors in the following categories: voice quality and tone, distance from the other person, body posture, eye contact, and the content of your speech. Examples of passive, assertive, and aggressive behaviors are provided to help you rate your own behaviors. Scores of 0 reflect assertive behaviors, and higher scores reflect greater passivity or aggression.

4. Next, total your score across all five categories. Your total score should range from 0 to 15. Scores closer to 0 are your goal, because they reflect assertive—not passive or aggressive—behaviors. Finally, give a subjective rating of how well you think the interaction turned out for you. That is, did you get what you wanted out of the interaction? Did you come across as firm and confident, yet respectful? If so, circle "great." If not, select the word that best describes how the interaction went for you.

5. Now, go back through your completed form and identify areas in which you could have been more assertive. For example, maybe your speech content was assertive, but you avoided making eye contact with the person. As you continue to interact with people and complete more forms, notice behaviors that repeatedly interfere with your assertiveness and make an extra effort to change these behaviors in future interactions. With continued practice, you will become more effective at handling interpersonal interactions—particularly those that have the potential for conflict. In so doing, you will get more of what you want in life, improve your relationships with others, and ultimately become less depressed.

We caution you that, like James, you may initially feel as though you are being mean or rude to other people. Although that is a possibility, it is probably not very likely. Remember that assertion is not the same as aggression.

Also, we warn you up front that people who have grown accustomed to your interpersonal behaviors may be somewhat surprised when you begin to assert yourself. In fact, they may even react somewhat negatively at first. The key here, though, is "at first." As they grow accustomed to your new level of assertiveness, they will likely respond to you more positively and more respectfully than they do now.

Worksheet: Overcoming Inhibitions

Date: _____

Briefly describe the situation, including with whom you interacted: _____

_____

_____

	Passive		Assertive		Aggressive	
Voice tone and quality	quiet, hesitant		clear, confident		shouting, harsh, threatening	
	3	2	1	0	1	2	3
Distance	far away		appropriately close		too close, in the other person's face	
	3	2	1	0	1	2	3
Body posture	slouched, facing away, hands fidgety or in pockets		relaxed, facing the person, hands relaxed or gesturing		arms crossed, muscles tensed, fists clenched	
	3	2	1	0	1	2	3
Eye contact	little to none		direct, but not staring		staring or glaring	
	3	2	1	0	1	2	3
Speech content	submissive, indirect		direct, respectful, firm		critical, accusatory, interrupting	
	3	2	1	0	1	2	3

Total score (0–15): _____

Subjective outcome: great   so-so   unsatisfactory

5 Learning Not to Sell Yourself Short

As we begin this chapter, let's take a look back at what you have done so far. You learned about depression and how it affects your life (chapter 1), you identified patterns of verbal and nonverbal behaviors in your interactions with others (chapter 2), you identified and are working to change your beliefs about your abilities in social settings (chapter 3), and you have begun working to assert yourself more when you interact with others (chapter 4). That alone is quite a lot, and we congratulate you for coming this far. However, there still remains much work to be done if you are to improve your relationships and conquer your depression.

In this chapter, we focus on a set of behaviors that resembles low assertiveness in that it involves the way you present yourself to others in social settings, yet this behavior differs in how you present yourself and in what circumstances. This behavior is selling yourself short, often referred to by mental health professionals as self-handicapping. Before we define self-handicapping and discuss how it is relevant to your depression, consider Mark Twain's advice: "Always acknowledge a fault. This will throw those in authority off their guard and give you an opportunity to commit more" (1999, 14). People who are depressed often put Mark Twain's witty advice into action, even in the absence of a fault—and unintentionally reap negative consequences.

SOCIAL EVALUATION AND SELF-HANDICAPPING

In chapter 4, we focused on your behaviors in situations that have the possibility for interpersonal conflict. In this chapter, we focus on your behaviors in a somewhat different context: *social evaluation,* or situations in which others are likely to form some impression or make some judgment about you and your abilities. Social evaluations can be as formal as a yearly performance evaluation at your job or as informal as a brief conversation about the clothes you are wearing.

Social evaluation can be difficult for many people, especially depressed people, because it holds the potential for rejection. That is, people's evaluations of you can be positive or negative, and if you are like most people who are depressed, your sensitivity to rejection has amplified with your depression. What's more, people's evaluations of you in one instance tend to determine their expectations of you at later times. For example, if you fail to hold up your end of the conversation on a first date, your partner is unlikely to expect that you will be a great conversationalist on a second date. Conversely, if you carry on a great conversation on the first date, your partner is likely to expect the same on the second.

So how do people behave in situations of social evaluation? Research indicates that people who are depressed are less likely than others to display defensive, self-enhancing behaviors in an effort to cast themselves in a favorable light (Alloy and Abramson 1982). In other words, when you are depressed, you tend to put forth less of an effort to make positive impressions on others, and you may be more quick to expose your faults to others. Interestingly, the same research indicates that nondepressed people actually overestimate their abilities and positive qualities at times. A slight dose of overoptimism can be healthy, but the experience of depression drains enough out of you that you no longer overestimate and actually begin to underestimate yourself.

Why do people sell themselves short in the presence of others? At face value, it seems like a behavior that would have only negative consequences. However, if people (including you) do it, then there must be some value in selling yourself short. Indeed, there is. Although it may seem contradictory at first, in a way, selling yourself short may protect you from the unpleasant consequences of negative social evaluations. Hang in there—we'll explain how.

What Is Self-Handicapping?

Self-handicapping, or selling yourself short, refers to placing obstacles in your path to success. This self-sabotage of sorts is done with the goal of providing an explanation of your performance in the event that you don't perform well (Leary and Shepperd 1986). That is, anticipating a possible failure or a poor performance of some kind, you may either claim to have some limitation or you may actually produce a limitation that provides an explanation for a poor performance. At times, self-handicapping may be intentional; at other times, you may do it without even realizing what you are doing. Either way, it's a way of providing an out when things go wrong. Let's look at a couple of examples.

Self-handicapping is by no means limited to people who are depressed. Consider, for example, a man in his late thirties who, under pressure from his coworkers, agrees to join the company softball team. Concerned with how others will evaluate his performance, he repeatedly mentions that "It's been years since I've held a bat" and "My back just isn't what it used to be." In the event that he plays poorly in the game, he (and others) can attribute his performance to a lack of recent practice and to back pain. On the other hand, if he plays well, he deserves extra praise because he did well in spite of the limitations. In this instance, the self-handicapping serves as a relatively benign way for him to reduce his concerns about social evaluation and to maintain his favorable self-image.

Now let's turn to a more extreme example. Consider a young woman who must pass an audition to gain admission to an honors music program at her university. Concerned about her ability to perform well in the honors program—and with others' evaluations of her if she does not—she occupies herself with other tasks and fails to prepare for the audition (note the connection here between procrastination and self-handicapping). Upon auditioning, she now has a ready explanation (she failed to prepare) if she performs poorly, and she appears all the more talented if she passes the audition despite not practicing. Notice that in this case, the young woman not only claims a handicap, as did the man in the earlier example, but also produces an actual handicap by not preparing for the audition.

Before we discuss the relevance of self-handicapping to your depression, let's review some of its general characteristics.

When Do People Self-Handicap?

Self-handicapping is common. People tend to sell themselves short in two kinds of situations (Baumgardner 1991). In the first, people self-handicap when they fail at something, no one else knows about it, and they don't want that failure to become public knowledge. This form of self-handicapping is called *claimed* or *self-reported* handicapping because no real handicap exists; it's just reported. Continuing our previous example of the man playing softball, perhaps he formerly played softball with a different group of people and repeatedly struck out. Based on that prior "failure," which is private in the sense that his current coworkers don't know about it, he may self-handicap so that a poor performance will not be attributed to a lack of skill on his part.

People also sell themselves short when they experience a success publicly yet doubt their ability to maintain that success. In this instance, they are likely to put forth less effort on tasks, procrastinate in preparing for or completing the task, or even do things that might sabotage their performance. This form of self-handicapping is called *acquired* or *behavioral* handicapping because an actual handicap is produced. Continuing the example of the woman who failed to prepare for her audition, perhaps she previously had success as a musician and received praise from others for her performances. Concerned that she will not be able to maintain her successful track record and will therefore lose the praise of others, she doesn't do much to prepare for her audition. Consequently, a poor performance will not be attributed to her abilities as a musician, but rather to her busy schedule and lack of adequate preparation.

In everyday life, claimed handicaps are more common than acquired handicaps. People's willingness to actually create handicaps for themselves depends on the interpersonal payoff of the handicaps. People claim handicaps when they believe that the handicap will explain their poor performance. People acquire handicaps, however, when they believe the handicap will explain their poor performance *and* lower others' future expectations.

EXERCISE 5.1:   Do You Sell Yourself Short?

So how does this relate to you? Thus far, we have talked on a very general level about "people" selling themselves short. As we will discuss later, it is likely that both claimed and acquired self-handicapping are relevant to your depression. Before we explore that issue, answer the following questions to get a clearer picture of the extent to which you sell yourself short.

		Check if yes
1.	Before making a presentation or speaking in a group (formally or informally), do you make statements indicating that something interferes with your ability to perform well (for example, you feel sick, you haven't practiced, the conditions aren't right)?	☐
2.	When people compliment you, do you then give an external reason for your success or downplay your role in the success (for example, "It was luck," "I didn't even try," "Anybody could have done it")?	☐
3.	Do you often qualify your statements with phrases such as "I don't know much about that," "I'm not really sure," or "I'm just guessing," when in reality you probably know as much or more about the topic than those around you?	☐
4.	Do you do things like the following that might make it harder for you to perform well or to succeed?	
	■ Procrastinate or wait until the last minute to finish things that will be evaluated by others	☐
	■ Fill your schedule with so many tasks that it is impossible for you to do any of them well	☐
	■ Drink or use other substances before evaluations such as tests, presentations, or first dates	☐
	Others:	☐
5.	Do you frequently turn down opportunities that truly interest you for fear that you won't succeed?	☐

6. List other possible ways in which you sell yourself short.	☐

Total score (number of checked boxes): _____

How did you score on that brief inventory? Higher scores reflect more self-handicapping. Some of the behaviors listed in exercise 5.1 can occur for reasons other than self-handicapping, of course. For example, it may be that your supervisor, not you, fills your schedule with so many tasks that you can't do any of them well. (If that's the case, then a review of the assertiveness exercises in chapter 4 may be helpful.) However, if several of the types of behaviors described in exercise 4.1 ring true for you, then you are probably self-handicapping. In the following sections, we explore some of the reasons for—and consequences of—selling yourself short.

Why Do People Self-Handicap?

Given that people claim and produce self-handicaps, and that you also may do so, let's turn to the question of why it happens. Explaining why behaviors happen is always tricky business, but selling yourself short is generally understood to be a way of protecting your self-esteem. As we said earlier, in situations where you perform poorly (and we all have those situations), self-handicapping reduces any threat to your self-esteem by providing an explanation as to why you didn't do well. In that sense, failures don't reflect poorly on your abilities or your worth as a person, but rather can be attributed to less threatening reasons such as low effort or a circumstance beyond your control. For example, if you set out to prepare a dessert for a dinner party and tell the guests that you decided to do it at the last minute and couldn't get all of the correct ingredients, you have provided an out if the dessert does not turn out well. That is, a bad dessert can be blamed on the last-minute preparation and missing ingredients rather than on your baking skills.

Jones and Berglas (1978) note that selling yourself short not only protects your self-esteem in the event of failure but also enhances your self-esteem when you succeed. For example, if the dessert turns out well, you deserve extra credit because you overcame the difficulties of last-minute preparation and made a good dessert even without all of the ingredients.

THE CONSEQUENCES OF SELLING YOURSELF SHORT

When you consider the protective and enhancing effects of self-handicapping, it appears to be a win-win behavior, right? You have an out if you fail, and you deserve extra praise if you succeed. So why not sell yourself short all the time?

Intuitively, it seems as though these behaviors would boost your self-esteem and reduce depression, rather than maintaining your depression or even making it worse. Unfortunately, that doesn't seem to be the case. Even though self-handicapping is done with the goal of promoting a more positive self-image, it ironically tends to have the opposite effect. There are a few possible reasons for this paradoxical effect.

First, other people in your social environment may not look favorably upon your efforts to sell yourself short. That then may lead to interpersonal friction or other difficulties in your relationships. An intriguing study by Rhodewalt and colleagues (1995) provides evidence for this. They found that others evaluated a person's performance more negatively when he made excuses about his performance. What's more, others evaluated the person's performance more negatively even when the performance was equal. That is, given the same performance by two people, the performance of the person who made excuses was evaluated more negatively than the performance of the person who did not make excuses. Therefore, the negative evaluation was unrelated to the person's actual performance, but rather resulted from the perception that he was making excuses for his performance.

Second, the short-term benefits of self-handicapping, like feeling less responsible for failures or feeling less pressure to succeed, tend to be outweighed by the long-term negative consequences. A fascinating example of this is seen in a study conducted by social psychologists Dianne Tice and Roy Baumeister (1997). They measured procrastination (a form of self-handicapping), stress, and health-related factors among college students at the beginning and the end of a semester. Interestingly, procrastinators were less likely than others to experience stress and illness at the beginning of the semester, but they experienced more stress and illness than others late in the semester. What's more, they received lower grades in the course and were ill more often during the semester. The immediate benefits of self-handicapping eventually give way to higher stress, poorer performance, and poorer health.

Finally, selling yourself short lowers others' expectations of you. While lower expectations may seem preferable at first, in that people are less demanding of you, the long-term consequences may be less desirable. Lower expectations engender lower opportunities. In this sense, self-handicapping leads to diminished demands and opportunities, which in turn makes it likely that you will underachieve or perform at levels below your abilities. As we said in chapter 4, reduced opportunities represent a form of loss, which serves as a trigger and a maintaining factor for your depression.

Consider the following interaction between Chris, who is depressed, and his therapist.

Chris: My boss offered to let me take the lead on the new project. Man, I couldn't believe it.

Therapist: Congratulations. How did you respond?

Chris: Well, I told her not to expect too much since it's not my specialty, and then she turned around and gave it to Rob because he has more experience in that area. Can you believe that?

Therapist: You seem surprised by that turn of events.

Chris: Yeah, I didn't think she would just up and change her mind like that. But it's probably for the best . . . I don't have enough energy these days to do that sort of thing, anyway.

Chris's self-handicapping led to the loss of a career-advancing opportunity, which further intensified his depressed mood. It was beneficial in the sense that it removed the immediate pressure associated with taking on greater job responsibilities. In the long run, however, the career damage and negative evaluations resulting from selling himself short served to maintain and increase his depressive symptoms.

Tying It In with Your Depression

In Chris's case, you saw how one instance of self-handicapping led to a loss of opportunity and an increase in depression. Is selling yourself short relevant to depression—and more importantly, is it relevant to you? Although self-handicapping has not been researched as extensively as some of the other behaviors discussed in this book (for example, social skills and reassurance seeking), evidence confirms that people are indeed more likely to sell themselves short when they are depressed. What's more, depressed people may self-handicap in a way that nondepressed people do not: they may use the very symptoms of their depression as handicaps (Baumgardner 1991; Rosenfarb and Aron 1992).

Consider the following conversation with William, a depressed patient who failed to complete a brief homework assignment that his therapist gave him in the previous session.

Therapist: What do you think might be interfering with your completing the homework assignment?

William: It's because I don't fall asleep until late, and then I'm so tired that I stay in bed till three or four in the afternoon.

Therapist: In our previous meeting, we talked about how you have tended to avoid trying things because you're concerned that others might judge you or see you as deficient. I wonder if that same pattern might be operating with regard to the homework assignment?

William: I don't think so . . . I really want to do them, but I'm sure I won't be able to do them well when I'm so tired.

Granted, William really did have difficulty sleeping at night, as do many depressed people. However, his ability to carry out the brief homework assignment was not contingent upon a full night's sleep. His reticence to complete the assignment seemed to stem more from his fear of social evaluation than from sleep problems, especially given that he tended to self-handicap in many areas of life. Interestingly, William did complete the homework assignment before the next session, but he noted that he could have done a better job on a full night's rest.

Turning to your depression now, can you think of instances in which depressive symptoms have served as a handicap to explain a poor performance? If so, under what circumstances does this typically occur? Respond to the questions in exercise 5.2 to get a better sense of whether you use depression to sell yourself short.

Exercise 5.2: Depressive Symptoms as Handicaps

Do you tell others that you are tired, fatigued, or sleep-deprived as a way to reduce their expectations for your performance? If the answer is yes, in what situations do you do that (for example, when your kids ask you to do something for them)?

_____

_____

_____

Do you indicate that you haven't been feeling well or that you are depressed when people present you with potential opportunities? If so, when and where does this typically happen?

_____

_____

_____

Do symptoms like fatigue and low energy lead you to procrastinate on starting or finishing tasks? List some specific instances in which this happens.

_____

_____

_____

Do you say things that express feelings of low self-esteem (for example, "I'm not good at that" or "I'll probably mess it up") before you do things for other people? What do you say, and when do you say it?

_____

_____

_____

Those questions tap into a few aspects of depression that can be used as self-handicaps: fatigue, tiredness, sadness, loss of interest, and feelings of worthlessness. Certainly, some of the other symptoms described in chapter 1 may also be used as handicaps. To the extent that you use these to sell yourself short, it may lead to a loss of opportunities and possibly even to negative reactions from others. Of course, it is important to recognize that depressive symptoms really do make it harder to perform well. We in no way mean that you somehow manipulate your depressive symptoms to get out of responsibilities. The issue is whether you present your depressive symptoms in a manner that reduces your opportunities to advance and to get what you want out of life.

■ Dante

Dante first came to our clinic accompanied by his wife (and at the behest of his wife), and he indicated a desire for help with his alcohol use. He believed that he did not have a "problem" with alcohol but that he occasionally drank a little too much. Upon further discussion, he revealed that he was in danger of losing his job in advertising because he had performed poorly at work or arrived late for work after nights of heavy drinking. It was at this point that his wife issued an ultimatum that he seek help or she would leave him. Dante somewhat grudgingly complied.

Dante drank only once or twice a week, but he drank heavily at those times, which happened to be on weeknights. As a result, he had great difficulty making it to work on time and adequately performing his work duties. In his job, Dante was required to make advertising presentations to potential clients—with a lot of money on the line at times. As Dante talked more about the specific circumstances under which his heavy drinking occurred, it became clear that he drank at night when he had an important presentation to make at work the following day. Dante reported that, despite success early in his career, he'd had a string of unsuccessful presentations in the past five years. After a few of these, he began drinking and staying out late on nights before important presentations.

Dante also had a few symptoms of depression. As it turned out, Dante met criteria for a diagnosis of dysthymia. Although he was unable to pinpoint the exact onset of his long-standing depression, his best estimate was that it started shortly after his decline at work but prior to his drinking problems.

Analysis

While Dante's drinking may have begun as a way of distracting himself and reducing anxiety about his upcoming presentations, it quickly evolved into a situation in which tying one on the night before became an explanation for his failures to secure contracts with potential clients. On the flip side, his infrequent successes were all the more impressive because he accomplished them in spite of being hungover. Although Dante's coworkers did not appreciate his behaviors and even made comments like "He could pull in so many contracts if he would lay off the bottle," it was easier for him to accept the notion that drinking interfered with his success than to entertain the thought that his salesmanship or presentational style were lacking. An important point here is that Dante didn't consider the possibility that his bids were unsuccessful due to factors unrelated to his presentations, such as lower estimates provided by competing advertising firms.

Dante's dysthymia fed into his self-handicapping, in that a primary characteristic of his dysthymia was low self-esteem. Unfortunately, his efforts to bolster his self-esteem by self-handicapping (that is, drinking before presentations) led to less success at work and a loss of respect from his coworkers. Further, he was on the verge of losing his job and possibly his wife.

To recover, Dante had to recognize the fear of negative social evaluation that drove his drinking and then take the risky step of opening himself up to such evaluations without having drinking as a fallback explanation. That was a step that took much work, but with encouragement and support from his wife, Dante took the step, learned to accept failure as a part of the business world (and not as something inherently wrong with him), and saw his success increase over time.

SELF-HANDICAPPING: AVOIDANCE IN DISGUISE

As we alluded to in the analysis of Dante's dilemma, self-handicapping can be understood as a form of disguised avoidance. The tendency to sell yourself short doesn't involve the trademark symptoms of avoidance, such as someone with a phobia of flying taking the bus across the country, but it does involve avoidance of the possibility of negative evaluations from others. In Dante's case, it was avoidance of his coworkers viewing him as a poor presenter, and his avoidance took the form of an acquired handicap (drinking) In your case, it may be avoidance of something entirely different, like avoidance of people thinking that you're not a good friend or avoidance of exposing your shortcomings to others. You may also use claimed handicaps rather than developing a handicap like drinking. Nonetheless, the same principle is at work when you offer a limitation as an explanation for poor performance. The key to overcoming this tendency, as we discuss in the next section, is confronting the fear of social evaluation and exposing yourself to the possibility of being viewed negatively.

CHALLENGE: PERFORM WITHOUT A HANDICAP

Now that you have a better understanding of what self-handicapping is and the extent to which you do it, we challenge you to go out on a limb and confront your fear of negative reactions from others. This will require that you first make yourself vulnerable to those reactions by performing without a handicap.

EXERCISE 5.3: Going Out on a Limb

Return to your responses to exercise 5.1, "Do You Sell Yourself Short?" After looking over your responses, select one of the situations or settings in which you self-handicap. If you are trying to decide between several options, we recommend an instance of procrastination as a good starting point.

If you don't have any instances of self-handicapping recorded there, carefully examine again whether you sell yourself short in any settings; most people do. If you still come up empty, consider enlisting assistance from someone who knows you well.

Using that specific handicap as a target, work during the next week to perform in a social setting without selling yourself short or procrastinating, as the case may be. That is, do the same thing that you normally do, but do it without making any excuses or giving any reasons why you might not perform well. If you engage in behavioral self-handicapping—that is, you behave in such a way as to set yourself up for a failure—make a concerted effort to stop that behavior. In the instance of procrastination, make completing the task your first priority.

The Going Out on a Limb worksheet may help provide structure to your efforts. Make several photocopies of the blank worksheet. We've provided a sample worksheet to help you get started.

    1.   On the sheet, record the date of the type of situation and the specific self-handicap that you want to target.

2. Now, based upon your knowledge of when you typically present that self-handicap, monitor yourself in that setting and situation.

3. After the situation has passed, describe the setting, what happened, and what you did. Stick to the facts here—just describe what happened, not what you thought or felt.

4. Then respond to the four items in the analysis section. Also record any feedback or responses that you receive from others.

After you have done this exercise several times, compare your behaviors and responses on the later forms to the earlier forms. What do you notice? Are you less likely to self-handicap? Do you see any patterns with regard to how successful your performances are? Remember, the goal here is not to simply be successful in your performance. The goal is to perform (whether well or poorly) without selling yourself short. Indeed, a second major component of this challenge is learning to accept both your good and bad performances in social settings. Both will happen. Nonetheless, as you learn to perform without handicapping yourself, your general level of success will increase, your level of worry and stress about performing will decrease, and you will receive more positive responses from others. As a result, you will begin to feel better about yourself, have better interpersonal relationships, and notice an improvement in your depression.

Worksheet: Going Out on a Limb

Date: _____

Briefly and specifically describe the handicap you're targeting: _____

_____

Briefly describe the situation: _____

_____

Analysis

1. Did you do the targeted self-handicapping behavior?   yes   no

2. Did you do other self-handicapping behaviors?   yes   no

3. Rate the success of your performance:

    unsuccessful   1   2   3   4   5   6   7   8   9   10   very successful

4. What did others say about your performance, if anything? _____

_____

_____

5. How did you feel during the performance? How do you feel now that you have finished it? _____

_____

_____

Sample Going Out on a Limb Worksheet

Date: _____6/23_____

Briefly and specifically describe the handicap you're targeting: ___Before I speak at a meeting, I often say that I was too busy to prepare anything for the meeting or to review the agenda prior to attending.___

Briefly describe the situation: ___I was attending the daily morning meeting. Amy asked me for my input on a problem we were to resolve.___

___I responded with my thoughts on the situation and did not qualify my statement with the comments that I normally make (or any other self-handicaps). Amy thanked me for my input, and the discussion shifted to the next item on the agenda.___

Analysis

1. Did you do the targeted self-handicapping behavior?   yes   (no)

2. Did you do other self-handicapping behaviors?   yes   (no)

3. Rate the success of your performance:

    unsuccessful   1   2   3   4   5   6   7   8   9   (10)   very successful

4. What did others say about your performance, if anything?   ___Amy thanked me for my input. Her response seemed positive.___
    ___Nobody else said anything.___

5. How did you feel during the performance? How do you feel now that you have finished it?   ___I felt nervous and vulnerable to___
    ___criticism while I was speaking. Now that it's over, I feel relieved, proud of myself for not making up an excuse, and more confident in my___
    ___ability   to   present   my   thoughts.___

Learning Not to Ask
for the Worst

By this point, we hope that you have identified situations in which you sell yourself short and that you are actively working to overcome that tendency. If you haven't begun to work on reducing your self-handicapping, we encourage you to revisit chapter 5 and make it a priority to target and change any instances in which you sell yourself short. Self-handicapping, as we discussed in chapter 5, involves presenting yourself to others as hindered or limited in some way that will interfere with your ability to succeed. In this chapter, we will examine negative feedback seeking, another social behavior that many people do when they are depressed. In contrast to self-handicapping, however, the social roles are reversed. That is, rather than portraying yourself to others as inadequate, you ask others to point out your faults.

WHAT IS NEGATIVE FEEDBACK SEEKING?

Negative feedback seeking, as the name implies, involves requesting that others evaluate or judge you negatively in some regard. For example, after painting a room in your house, you might ask your spouse what she doesn't like about the shade of paint you used, rather than asking if she likes what you have done. In the following paragraphs, we review what negative feedback seeking is, then we discuss why people do it.

Seeking feedback about yourself from others, either positive or negative, is a natural part of social interaction. We all do it, and it can take the form of anything from asking your friend if she likes your new shirt to asking your spouse if she thinks you are a good parent. It can be asking a fellow soccer player if he thinks you are a good defender or a lousy defender. Seeking feedback is normal, healthy, and even necessary to maintain good social relations.

Exercise 6.1: What Do You Seek Feedback About?

To get a better sense of the circumstances in and topics about which you routinely seek feedback from others, complete this brief exercise.

List some situations in which you often ask others their opinion about your characteristics or qualities (for example, asking a friend about your hair or asking a coworker about your job performance).

_____

_____

_____

Where and when do you usually ask for this feedback (for example, during a lunch break at work or while sitting at home in the evenings)?

_____

_____

_____

Now that you are primed and thinking about when and what you ask others to give you feedback, let's delve a little deeper into the nature of feedback seeking. Based on the knowledge that all humans seek feedback in social settings, social psychologist William Swann (1990) developed a theory to explain such behaviors. He labeled it *self-verification theory*, and in it, he proposed that people's primary goal when they seek feedback from others is to maintain predictable, certain, and familiar self-concepts. In other words, you ask people to evaluate you in order to keep a steady sense of who you are. To do this, you actively seek responses from others that are consistent with the way you already view yourself. For example, if you hold the belief that you are a lousy cook, then you will likely feel a certain amount of connection to others who share and validate your belief rather than contradict your belief. In real life, it might go something like this:

I think I'm a lousy cook. Jennifer agrees that I'm a lousy cook. Jennifer really knows me and is honest with me.

Now consider the reverse scenario, in which someone gives you a response that is not consistent with your view of yourself:

I think I'm a lousy artist. Joseph says I'm a good artist. Joseph either doesn't know me well or isn't being honest with me.

As you can see from these two short examples, it's natural to be inclined to accept others' feedback and opinions about you when they coincide with your own beliefs about yourself and to dismiss and reject others' comments about you when they contradict your beliefs about yourself. At this point, you might be thinking that this all seems logical and makes perfect sense. However, there is a surprising catch. A key component of this theory is that there is no difference in self-verification needs between people with positive self-concepts and people with negative self-concepts. In other words, people who think favorably of themselves and people who think poorly of themselves all need feedback from others that is consistent with their self-views. An implication of this, and the part that can seem surprising, is that people with negative self-views actually want others to give them negative feedback that agrees with their self-views.

Interestingly, you are probably very accustomed to people desiring positive responses from others; it seems somehow normal when people desire warmth, praise, and positive evaluations. If we were to ask you right now if most people would rather have a person say something good about them or something bad about them, your immediate response would probably be to go with the good feedback. And, according to self-verification theory, it is normal to desire positive feedback, because most people have positive self-concepts. For people with positive self-concepts, confirming their sense of self involves seeking warmth, praise, and so on.

By the same token, people with negative self-concepts also desire self-confirmation, but in their case, this means seeking criticism and other negative responses from those around them. This is negative feedback seeking. Swann and his colleagues (1992) suggest that people with negative self-concepts are motivated to do this even at the cost of receiving unpleasant feedback. That is, even though it might not feel good in some ways to receive negative appraisals from others, the need for self-verification is so strong that people with negative self-concepts will continue to ask for the worst.

Do People Really Ask for Negative Feedback?

If you're having trouble buying into the notion that people actually seek out negative evaluations from others, that's okay. It does seem contrary to our general human nature of preferring compliments to criticism. However, it's not that some people prefer unfavorable evaluations in a masochistic sense that they derive pleasure from it; in fact, they find it quite unpleasant. In spite of the painful emotional consequences of receiving negative feedback, it seems that people with negative self-concepts still gravitate toward it because they view it as sincere, genuine, and reflective of who they really are.

Several research studies document that people with low self-esteem really do ask for the worst. For example, Giesler, Josephs, and Swann (1996) set up an experiment in which they determined each participant's level of self-esteem. Then all participants, whatever their level of self-esteem, were presented with a choice: they could interact with an interviewer who tended to provide warm feedback, an interviewer who tended to provide somewhat critical feedback, or an interviewer who was relatively neutral. Among participants with a positive self-concept, a huge majority elected to chat with the interviewer who tended to be warm and positive. Among those with a negative self-concept, however, a substantial proportion elected to see the negative interviewer, despite the equal availability of other, less negative interviewers. When asked about their choice, these participants often responded that they believed the negative interviewer was likely to understand them more fully and accurately.

So, it appears that people with low self-concepts do indeed ask for the worst from others. In the next section, we will discuss reasons why that may be the case. But before we talk more about why people seek negative feedback and how it is important to understanding your depression, complete exercise 6.2 to see if you, too, ask for the worst.

EXERCISE 6.2:   Do You Ask for the Worst?

	Check one:	+	−
1.	Imagine that you just made a performance about which others will give you feedback. It could be an athletic event, a musical performance, food you prepared, a presentation you gave, and so on. Think of a performance that is most relevant to you. When you talk with friends or family members after the performance, would you rather they tell you what was good about your performance (+) or what was bad about your performance (−)?	☐	☐
2.	With regard to your physical appearance, would you prefer for someone to tell you what features make you attractive (+) or what features make you unattractive (−)?	☐	☐
3.	Imagine that you are having a conversation about what qualities make someone a good friend. Would you rather your conversation partner tell you which of those qualities you possess (+) or which of those qualities you lack (−)?	☐	☐

4. Would you rather someone close to you tell you why she thinks you are smart (+) or why she thinks you are of average to below-average intelligence (–)?	☐	☐
5. Imagine that you have just gone on a date. If you had to choose between your date describing what he or she views as your best conversational skills (+) or your worst conversational skills (–), which would you choose?	☐	☐
6. Imagine that you and your acquaintances were asked to make a list of each other's strengths and weaknesses. If you were only allowed to see one list about yourself, would you choose to see the list of your strengths (+) or the list of your weaknesses (–)?	☐	☐
Total number of boxes checked in each column:		

After you have finished responding to the questions in this exercise, add up the number of positive answers and the number of negative answers. If you selected all or almost all positives, then you probably aren't seeking much negative feedback at the moment. However, if you checked two or more negative responses, then it's likely that you are asking others around you to negatively evaluate you. We will discuss the potential consequences of doing that later in this chapter. For now, let's turn to the question of why people—perhaps including you—ask for the worst.

WHY DO PEOPLE ASK FOR THE WORST?

What exactly are people up to when they seek self-confirming feedback? What specifically motivates them? As we mentioned earlier, a sense of familiarity, predictability, and control is no doubt one important motivation for seeking negative feedback from others. That is, even if it is negative, your self-concept is your self-concept, and any changes to it are likely to rock the boat. If you radically changed your self-views, it would take a lot of getting used to, both for you and for the people around you who are used to your old self.

Imagine that you are somewhat shy and typically lack confidence in social settings. If you were to suddenly transform into a socially confident, assertive, and outgoing person, it would drastically alter your behaviors around others and your sense of who you are. Likewise, your friends, family members, and coworkers, who have grown accustomed to the unassertive and socially unconfident you, would be forced to change how they interact with you and how they view you. When you consider all the change and rough transitions that would come about through changing your self-concept, it's no wonder that people tend to seek out feedback that is consistent with their self-concept, even if that means asking for the worst.

The Important Role of Self-Esteem

Throughout this chapter, we have used phrases such as "self-concept," "self-views," and "beliefs about yourself," and we've suggested that these play a role in asking for the worst. These terms are simply different ways of referring to your self-esteem. Self-esteem is the driving mechanism behind feedback seeking. That is, the extent to which your self-esteem is positive or negative determines the extent to which you ask for feedback that is positive or negative. If, on the one hand, your self-esteem is mostly positive, then you will primarily look for positive evaluations. If, on the other hand, you hold a negative view of yourself, then you are more likely to look for and accept negative feedback that confirms your view.

It's natural for your self-esteem to vary over time given certain situations or settings, and as your self-esteem changes, your feedback seeking is also likely to change. In our own research, we found that the experience of a stressful life event led to lower self-esteem, which in turn led people to seek more negative feedback (Pettit and Joiner 2001b). One implication of this is that when you are most "stressed out" or have experienced a setback (for example, the ending of a romantic relationship or the loss of a job), then your self-esteem will probably decrease temporarily, and you will probably seek more negative feedback as a result of the drop in self-esteem.

We expect that at this point, you may be skeptical. That is, you may be thinking that if things are bad and your self-esteem is low, then it would be better to be "deceived" with positive feedback from others. For example, you might think, *If I'm feeling crummy about myself, wouldn't it help me out and make me feel better if the people around me said nice things about me? Surely I'd be better off if they complimented me on all my positive qualities, even if they aren't sincere.* That position certainly seems to make sense at first glance, and we can understand if you're thinking that way. Nevertheless, our research suggests that it's not that straightforward.

Feedback Seeking and Symptoms of Depression and Anxiety

Studies among college roommates (Joiner and Kistner 2004) assessed the degree to which their views of themselves corresponded with their roommates' views of them. The degree of correspondence between the roommates' views was related to the students' depressed and anxious symptoms. That is, students whose roommate's beliefs about them matched their own beliefs about themselves experienced fewer symptoms of depression and anxiety, while those whose roommate's beliefs about them differed from their own had higher levels of depressive and anxious symptoms.

It is not surprising that students who viewed themselves positively and were viewed by roommates positively would have low depression and anxiety. What was surprising was that correspondences of any type seemed to relate to well-being, and discordances of any type were associated with higher levels of symptoms. That is, the people with negative self-concepts seemed to be protected from symptoms if their roommates confirmed their negative self-views. This finding implies that feedback consistent with a person's own self-image, regardless of whether it is positive or negative, is soothing and feedback that conflicts with a person's own self-image, even if it is positive, is unsettling.

Could this be true? Is it the case that asking for and receiving negative feedback about yourself is a good thing that promotes your well-being? Maybe in a very limited and short-term manner, but in general, that doesn't appear to be the case, either. Consider Debbie's story.

■ Debbie

Debbie came to our clinic seeking help with her feelings of depression. She reported difficulty staying asleep during the night, fatigue during the day, and feelings of sadness, worthlessness, and guilt (even though she had difficulty pinpointing exactly what she felt guilty about). Of even greater concern, she had thoughts that she would be better off dead than alive, and she occasionally thought about ways that she might end her life. Each of those is a relatively common symptom of depression, and their occurrence for at least two weeks indicated that Debbie was in the midst of a major depressive episode.

After we talked further, it became clear that this was not Debbie's first bout of depression. Indeed, she had experienced several distinct periods, or episodes, of major depression. She would typically go two to four years with few or no depressive symptoms (other than the occasional rough day that everyone experiences), then would feel herself slipping into what she described as a "funk." Her "funks," which were episodes of major depression, usually lasted for five or six months, then tended to gradually go away. Debbie said she felt sure that her current depressive episode would also go away eventually, but she wanted to put an end to the pattern of drifting in and out of depression. In her own words, she wanted to "beat it once and for all."

Not all depressed people are alike; quite to the contrary, many people with many different ways of acting and thinking experience depression. Debbie wasn't shy and didn't usually avoid interpersonal conflict. She liked to think of herself as a straight shooter, and that was an accurate description of her most of the time. However, Debbie did often sell herself short when she was around others. This was consistent with her general low self-esteem.

Granted, she didn't have low self-esteem in all areas of her life. For example, she worked as an acquisitions manager and felt very confident that she was good at her job. Nevertheless, there were many ways in which she felt very poorly about herself, including her physical appearance and her ability to maintain friendships. In fact, it was typically in these areas that Debbie would sell herself short and make derogatory comments about herself. For example, when she first came for treatment, she jokingly remarked that she didn't want to sit down too quickly for fear that the chair would break because of her weight.

Consistent with her tendency to belittle herself and her abilities, Debbie often sought negative feedback from others. She also found it difficult to accept compliments. She said that compliments made her uncomfortable and that she didn't know what to say or do when others gave her positive feedback. In contrast, she viewed criticisms as more sincere and stated that at least she knew where she stood around people who gave her negative feedback.

Debbie's tendency to pull for negative responses from others also became apparent in her interactions with her therapist. Consider the following discussion in one of her therapy sessions:

Debbie: I'm not a friendly person. I've never been easy to get along with; there's really nothing nice about me.

Therapist: *(looking doubtful)* Hmm . . .

Debbie: It's true.

Therapist: I'm not sure I see it.

Debbie: People don't think I'm nice; only those who can tolerate a lot like me. This is true.

Therapist: I'm still not sure I see it.

Debbie: Well, perhaps you will . . . You know, there is no need to make me feel better. I just want you to be honest.

Intentionally or unintentionally, Debbie tried to pull the therapist to see things her way. When the therapist remained neutral, this only intensified Debbie's wish to persuade her. Of course, there is nothing unusual about attempting to persuade others, but Debbie's efforts at persuasion were geared toward making herself look worse.

Analysis

First, note that if you, like Debbie, have thoughts of ending your life, we strongly urge you to seek out help from a mental health professional. This book is designed to help you overcome your depression, but there are times when professional help is necessary.

Debbie clearly had low self-esteem and felt poorly about herself in many ways. Her low self-esteem served as the driving force behind her tendency to ask for the worst from others. She had great difficulty accepting positive comments made about her and consequently avoided being around people who praised her. Rather, she found it easier to accept derogatory statements from others and even to make such statements about herself.

So how was this related to her depression? The problem with negative feedback, frankly, is that it rarely makes people feel good. And that was the case with Debbie. One the one hand, she felt more at ease with negative feedback because it seemed sincere to her. On the other hand, the negative comments still hurt. For example, critical comments about Debbie's weight worsened her own insecurities and views about her appearance. Likewise, when others confirmed Debbie's view that she was hard to get along with, she felt even sadder and wondered why she wasn't more upbeat and cordial. In short, Debbie rejected the very feedback that might make her feel better about herself, and she asked for feedback that made her feel worse.

Treatment with Debbie focused on helping her to recognize her pattern of asking for the worst and rejecting the positive, helping to modify her low self-esteem that drove this pattern of behavior, and helping her learn to intentionally ask for and accept positive feedback. Although it was not easy for Debbie to change her long-standing pattern of asking for the worst, she gradually did so with repeated practice. As a result, her self-esteem improved, her social relationships improved, and she felt less vulnerable to future episodes of depression.

DISMISSING THE POSITIVE

In addition to asking for the worst, Debbie engaged in another interpersonal behavior when she was depressed: she dismissed others' compliments and praise as inaccurate or insincere. This is consistent with the tendency to ask for the worst, although it represents your response to others rather than your requests of them. While requesting that others provide you with negative feedback certainly has negative implications for your relationships, it's important that you also consider your response to others' feedback.

So what is the effect of dismissing, minimizing, or rejecting others' positive feedback? These sorts of responses not only emphasize your low self-esteem but also tend to push people away by giving the impression that you don't appreciate their genuinely positive opinions about you. In order to improve your self-esteem, reduce your depression, and have better relationships with others, you must stop seeking negative feedback from them, and you must also accept their positive feedback. How do you do that? It's amazing how effectively a smile, direct eye contact, and a "thank you" can improve the tone of a conversation. Consider the following examples of dismissing and accepting positive feedback:

Your friend:	You've done a great job fixing your place up. It looks much better than when you moved here. You have a knack for decorating.
You, dismissing the positive:	Not really, I just copied what I saw in a magazine. And if you look closely, you'll see that the colors don't even match.

You, accepting   Thanks, I worked hard to get it the way I wanted it to look.
the positive:

Notice the difference in the tone that the two responses set for the remainder of the conversation. In the first situation, your friend is stuck with two choices: argue with you about why your house looks good or agree that you didn't do a good job of decorating your house. What often happens is that this type of dismissive response creates a sense of discomfort and tension, stifling the conversation. In contrast, when you accept your friend's compliment, you are expressing that you appreciate the comment and that you agree. The conversation can then naturally continue as a discussion of decorating your house or flow into a different topic. In this sense, your responses to others' positive comments play an important role in determining how well you get along with them—and, consequently, how you feel.

EXERCISE 6.3:   Do You Dismiss the Positive?

The scenario above was purely hypothetical. How do you respond to others in real life? Do you dismiss positive remarks made by others? Answer these questions to determine the extent to which you dismiss the positive.

	Yes	No
1. Do you feel uncomfortable, feel tense, or wish you could escape when others say nice things about you?	☐	☐
2. When people compliment your performance (for example, at work, at school, or about the way you dress), do you often respond with minimizing comments such as "It was luck," "I won't be able to do it again," "This is the only good thing I do," or "Just wait till you know me better"?	☐	☐
3. When people give you positive feedback, do you often think that they are insincere, perhaps just trying to be nice to you?	☐	☐
4. Do you avoid situations in which you might receive praise, compliments, or expressions of gratitude? (For example, would you leave a gift for someone rather than give it to them in person because you might feel uncomfortable when they thank you? Do you avoid ceremonies in which you may be honored?)	☐	☐
Total number of boxes checked in each column:		

When you add up your yes and no responses, do you see any examples of dismissing the positive in your life? If you answered yes to one or more, then you are probably dismissing the positive at least some of the time. If that is the case, then take a moment to list specific situations where you have dismissed the positive.

_____

_____

_____

_____

We will return to dismissing the positive—and your specific instances of doing it—later in this chapter. Before we do that, however, let's examine the consequences of asking for the worst.

BE CAREFUL WHAT YOU ASK FOR . . . AND WHAT HAPPENS IF YOU GET IT

Earlier in this chapter, we raised the question of whether asking for negative feedback could have a positive effect since it promotes a sense of consistency and predictability. As was the case with Debbie, however, the "benefit" of asking for the worst is very short-lived. Instead, what tends to happen is that people feel worse after they receive negative feedback. In fact, several researchers have found that people who tend to ask for the worst—and then receive it—are at an increased risk of becoming more depressed.

Much of the work in this area has been done by social psychologist William Swann and his colleagues (Swann et al. 1992; Swann, Wenzlaff, and Tafarodi 1992). They have found that people who are depressed are more likely than others to seek negative feedback. What's more, depressed people who seek negative feedback are more likely to be rejected by others. One interpretation of these findings is that depressed people are rejected more often because they tend to gravitate to people who evaluate them negatively. For example, a depressed man with low self-esteem who seeks negative feedback is more likely to become romantically involved with women who also hold him in low esteem. As a result, he is more likely to experience hostile, dismissive responses from these women, which will in turn leave him feeling even more depressed.

We conducted two studies that demonstrated that people who express an interest in negative feedback and who receive it are vulnerable to increases in depressive symptoms (Joiner 1995; Pettit and Joiner 2001a). Thus, there is growing evidence that people with depressive symptoms actively ask for the worst, often receive it, and may become even more depressed as a result. Sadly, a cycle can be established in which people who are depressed ask for the worst, then feel more depressed and have even lower self-esteem after they receive the worst, and then are even more likely to continue to ask for the worst.

Tying It In with Your Depression

By now, you are probably starting to understand why people ask for the worst and what happens when they receive it. How does this apply to you? Well, if you are depressed, there is a good chance that you are engaging in at least some negative feedback seeking. It may be with friends, coworkers, roommates, or your family. Although you may feel that others are being more sincere when they make comments that confirm your own negative views of yourself, and you may find this negative feedback easier to accept because it seems true, it's also probably the case that you feel sad or hurt by those comments. That is, those comments ultimately make you feel worse about yourself and intensify your depression. As a result, you may be caught in the cycle of low self-esteem, negative feedback seeking, and depression. If so, what can you do to stop it?

CHALLENGE: DEVELOP A MORE POSITIVE VIEW OF YOURSELF

While actually stopping the cycle will take hard work, the "how" is relatively straightforward. Recall that your self-esteem is what determines the extent to which you seek positive or negative feedback. That is, you'll look for positive feedback if you feel good about yourself, and you'll ask for the worst if you feel bad about yourself. With that knowledge, then, a key to stopping the cycle of negative feedback seeking and depression is to develop a more positive view of yourself. *But how do I do that?* you may be thinking. *I've been this way all my life. How can I suddenly change how I feel about myself?*

Step 1: Do Something Fun

We agree that it's not easy, and we in no way want to suggest that you overhaul your entire self-concept overnight. Rather, positive change will come about through a more gradual process that requires effort and repeated practice. Nevertheless, there are ways in which you can temporarily change your mood and self-concept. For example, in one of our studies, we found that people's self-esteem dropped after they experienced a stressful life event (Pettit and Joiner 2001b). The converse is that experiencing pleasant events is likely to at least temporarily make your mood and self-esteem more positive. Now, we're not talking about events like winning the lottery; rather, we are referring to relatively minor things that you can do to put yourself in a more positive mood.

One of the side effects of depression is that people often stop doing things that they enjoy. The first step in stopping the cycle of asking for the worst is to start doing things that you enjoy. This is obviously different for every person, but examples of fun things to do might include going to a movie, taking a walk in a park, reading an intriguing novel, chatting with a friend with whom you haven't spoken in a while, or treating yourself to a meal at your favorite restaurant. Don't just take these examples and simply follow them like a prescription; make sure to select things that you really enjoy. A second piece of advice for this exercise: don't become preoccupied with finding the best possible activity. Remember, the goal is to start doing the little things again, not to take on huge tasks and activities that leave you feeling more stressed out than relaxed.

Once you have identified some fun, easy-to-do activities, make it a priority to do them regularly. While this alone may not be a long-term solution to depression, it will probably help you feel somewhat less depressed and feel better about yourself. As a result, you will be less focused on the negative and less likely to ask for the worst.

Step 2: Stop Asking for the Worst

Okay, now on to step 2. Completing step 1 will likely help reduce negative feedback seeking, but it probably won't stop it entirely, especially if you have been doing it for a long time. Therefore, a second key to overcoming negative feedback seeking is to make an intentional effort to stop looking for negative feedback. This may seem simplistic, but it is important. Now that you understand what negative feedback seeking is and have examined situations in which you do it, you must fight your tendencies to ask for and accept negative evaluations from others. For example, if you normally tell your spouse or close friend about mistakes you've made and get responses such as "Yeah, you messed that up" or "That was a dumb thing to do," make it a point to tell them about something good you did, or at least something neutral. In so doing, you will likely receive feedback that is neutral or even positive, which brings us to step 3.

Step 3: Accept the Positive

Doing something fun (step 1) and putting an end to asking for the worst (step 2) will take you part of the way to ending the cycle of negative feedback seeking and depression. To complete the process, there remains one thing to do: accept positive feedback when others give it to you. Like Debbie, you may feel uncomfortable when others praise you or compliment you. You may even find ways of minimizing or dismissing their praise. For example, you may respond to compliments with statements such as "It was luck" or "Yeah, but you should have seen how I messed up the other day." To stop the cycle of negative feedback seeking and depression, you must learn to accept others' positive statements about you.

Now that you understand the three steps to stopping the cycle of asking for the worst and feeling depressed, it's time to put them into action. This exercise will help you to do that.

EXERCISE 6.4:   Changing the Filter

Step 1: Do Something Fun

In the space provided below, list at least five activities that you enjoy. Make sure that these are activities that you can readily do without a large investment of time and energy. For example, you may really enjoy snow skiing. If you live several hours from the nearest ski slope, however, you will have very limited opportunities to go skiing. Rather, list activities that you can (relatively) easily do without much preparation (for example, seeing a movie, taking a walk, or having coffee or tea with a friend).

Activity   **Day and Time**

_____   _____

_____   _____

_____   _____

_____   _____

_____   _____

Choose one of the activities that you have listed above, and in the space beside it, write down a day and a time when you will do that activity. Make it within the next few days, not several weeks down the road. After you have done that activity, select another one from the list, and choose a day and a time when you will do it. Follow that procedure for each of the activities you have listed, and be faithful in doing them when you say you will.

Step 2: Stop Asking for the Worst

For a moment, return to exercise 6.1. After reviewing your responses to those questions, select one situation in which you often ask others for negative feedback. When you are in that situation (or a similar one) over the next week, focus on maintaining the topic of that conversation on a positive or neutral theme. If you feel the urge to make a self-deprecating remark or ask about some negative quality of yourself, work to shift the conversation in a different direction. Then try the same thing with the other situations you listed in exercise 6.1.

Step 3: Accept the Positive

To complete step 3, return to exercise 6.3. Select an instance in which you downplay, minimize, or outright reject others' positive comments about you. When you are in that situation (or a similar one) over the coming week, resist your normal response of dismissing the positive. Instead, respond in a manner that expresses appreciation and affirms the person's statements (for example, "Thank you"). If positive feedback does not occur naturally in the course of conversations during the next week, then take it upon yourself to ask somebody for positive feedback. This is not self-serving, and it can often be done without others realizing what you are doing. For example, you might ask people what they like about something you did. Suppose you complete a project at work or school. You might ask your boss or professor to tell you what she thinks are the strengths of your project. If you cook a meal and eat it with your roommates, you might ask what they thought was the best part of the meal. This will bring about positive feedback, and you can then practice accepting it instead of rejecting it.

7 Becoming Self-Assured

Throughout this book, we have highlighted the idea that you may tend to withdraw from others when you are depressed. And while this is often true on a broad level of social interactions, like at work, at school, or with acquaintances, it isn't the case that most depressed people completely cut off relationships. A more common pattern is for depressed people to depend on a few close relationships to meet their needs for social connectedness and interpersonal warmth. Reflect for a moment upon your own relationships. Is it the case that you become less engaged in inter-personal activities on the whole when you are depressed, but you maintain a small number of very close relationships? If so, then your needs for social connection are probably concentrated in your relationships with only a few people.

Maintaining close relationships is important for a number of reasons. However, having very few close relationships can sometimes lead to an overreliance on one person to meet your social and emotional needs. When that happens, two consequences are likely. First, your significant other (be it a spouse, romantic partner, friend, or family member) can become burdened with fulfilling all of your needs for social interaction, and that may eventually strain your relationship. Second, and more importantly, overreliance on one person places you in a precarious position. If something disrupts your relationship, you are left socially isolated.

When your close relationships are strained and you have no alternative sources for social interaction, the unfortunate result is that you may become depressed. This notion is supported by research which indicates that people who rely heavily on a single relationship to meet their social and emotional needs are in jeopardy of becoming depressed when that source is disrupted (American Psychiatric Association 1994). In extreme and prolonged cases, this behavior may represent *dependent personality disorder,* described as a "pervasive and excessive need to be taken care of that leads to submissive and clinging behavior and fears of separation . . ." (American Psychiatric Association 1994, 668).

It is important to recognize that dependent personality disorder and depression are not the same thing, and we encourage you not to diagnose yourself with dependent personality disorder. Nevertheless, it is true that many people who are depressed interact with others in ways that resemble features of dependence. For example, one sign of interpersonal dependence is difficulty expressing disagreement with others. As we discussed at length in chapter 4, avoidance of interpersonal conflict is common when you are depressed, and it can play a role in maintaining your depression.

We hope that you have done the exercises in chapter 4 and are working toward becoming more assertive in your social interactions. Besides avoidance of conflict, are there other areas in your life that suggest interpersonal dependence? Exercise 7.1 will help you examine the extent to which you have trouble with interpersonal dependence, or relying too much on one relationship.

EXERCISE 7.1:   Signs of Interpersonal Dependence

Circle the number below each question that best describes your answer. Then add up your answers to obtain a total score.

1. Do you find it uncomfortable to be alone because you are concerned that you might not be able to take care of yourself?

    never   1   2   3   4   5   always

2. Is it hard for you to start activities or projects on your own because you believe you might not be capable of completing them (not because you are tired or lacking energy)?

    never   1   2   3   4   5   always

3. Do you find it difficult to express disagreement with others because you are concerned that they may disapprove of you or withdraw their friendship from you?

    never   1   2   3   4   5   always

4. Is it hard for you to make everyday decisions (for example, where to eat dinner, what to watch on TV, or what clothes to wear) without advice and reassurance from others?

    never   1   2   3   4   5   always

5. Do you agree to or volunteer to do things you don't enjoy so that others will not be disappointed with you (for example, taking on extra work, cleaning the apartment so your roommate doesn't have to)?

never   1   2   3   4   5   always

Total: _____

Do your responses in exercise 7.1 reveal aspects of your interpersonal relationships that you hadn't considered before? A higher total score reflects greater interpersonal dependence. Does your score suggest that you rely heavily upon significant others? If so, that reliance may play a role in maintaining your depression.

Don't misunderstand us—close relationships are very important. Indeed, this book is based upon the premise that improving your relationships with others will improve your depression. The key is that overreliance on a limited number of relationships for support, as well as specific ways of interacting with people in those relationships (such as negative feedback seeking and excessive reassurance seeking), may actually make your depressive symptoms worse and make them last longer. How might it do that? The answer to that question is probably complex, but certain things you say and do may inadvertently strain your relationships and leave you feeling isolated and rejected. The good news is that by recognizing and changing those specific behaviors, you can improve the quality of your relationships and help break the cycle of depression.

In the remainder of this chapter, we will examine one particular interpersonal behavior that is intertwined with dependence and depression: *excessive reassurance seeking.*

WHAT IS EXCESSIVE REASSURANCE SEEKING?

Excessive reassurance seeking, in a sense, can be thought of as going to the interpersonal well too many times. Stated another way, excessive reassurance seeking is the tendency to excessively seek assurances from others that you are lovable and worthy, and to persist in the asking even after such assurance has already been provided. Consider the following conversation between Eddie and his girlfriend, Sylvia.

Eddie: You seem bored. Do you enjoy talking with me like this?

Sylvia: Of course I enjoy it. Why would you think I don't?

Eddie: Well, you seemed like you weren't into the conversation or you just wanted it to end. That made me start to wonder if you really enjoy when we talk. Do you?

Sylvia: Sure I enjoy our conversations. I wouldn't be with you if I didn't.

Eddie: Really? You're not just saying that, right?

Sylvia: No, Eddie.

Eddie: I don't know . . . It just seemed like you were getting bored listening to me talk. Deep down inside, are you starting to get tired of me?

Sylvia: (*exasperated*) What is it with you, Eddie? I already told you how I feel. You can either believe me or not.

Did you get the sense that Eddie simply couldn't be satisfied that Sylvia truly cares about him and likes him, no matter how much she insisted? Eddie wanted Sylvia to tell him that she enjoys talking with him, but he also had great difficulty accepting her assurances.

EXERCISE 7.2:   Your Reaction to Eddie and Sylvia

Before we explain some potential consequences of excessive reassurance seeking, answer the following questions about your reaction to Eddie and Sylvia's conversation.

Do you identify with Eddie's dilemma? That is, do you often feel as though you want others to tell you that you are important to them, but then don't feel entirely satisfied when they do? If so, in what relationships does that happen?

_____

_____

_____

What was your first reaction to what Eddie said? If you were in Sylvia's position, what would you think about Eddie?

_____

_____

_____

If you see some of your own tendencies in Eddie's behaviors, then you're not alone. Interactions just like Eddie and Sylvia's led psychologist Jim Coyne (1976) to develop a theory of how people may become depressed. He proposed that when you experience doubts about your own worth and whether others truly care about you, you may seek reassurance from them. Others may provide reassurance, but with little effect, because you doubt the reassurance, attributing it instead to others' sense of pity or obligation. You thus face a very difficult problem: you both need and doubt others' reassurance. The need for reassurance is emotionally powerful, and as a result, it may win out (at least temporarily), compelling you to again go back to the well for reassurance from others. Even if you receive it, however, you again doubt the reassurance, and the pattern is repeated. The result is a cycle of needing reassurance, asking for reassurance, then dismissing the reassurance once it is provided. Does this sound like a familiar pattern in your relationships? If so, then you are probably seeking reassurance excessively.

EXERCISE 7.3:   Assessing Your Reassurance Seeking

To get a better sense of whether this is happening in your life, let's examine the extent to which you seek reassurance from others. Circle the number below each question that is most appropriate to you. Then add up the numbers you circled to calculate your total score.

1. In general, do you often find yourself asking the people you feel close to how they truly feel about you?

    not at all   1   2   3   4   5   very much

2. In general, do you frequently seek reassurance from the people you feel close to as to whether they really care about you?

    not at all   1   2   3   4   5   very much

3. In general, do the people you feel close to sometimes become irritated with you for seeking reassurance from them about whether they really care about you?

    not at all   1   2   3   4   5   very much

4. In general, do the people you feel close to sometimes get fed up with you for seeking reassurance from them about whether they really care about you?

    not at all   1   2   3   4   5   very much

Total: _____

How did you score on exercise 7.3? Higher scores reflect higher levels of reassurance seeking. If you answered 2, 3, or 4 on some items, then it's likely that you are seeking reassurance and that it may have a negative impact on your personal relationships.

Is Reassurance Seeking a Bad Thing?

But is reassurance seeking necessarily bad? Certainly, everyone desires comfort and assurances from time to time. We have been careful to use the word "excessive" to emphasize a key distinction between extreme reassurance seeking and general social support. Social support is healthy and reduces the likelihood that you will become depressed. But there is a big difference between the healthy search for social support and the repeated and persistent seeking of reassurance from the same person, even after it has already been provided.

CONSEQUENCES OF EXCESSIVE REASSURANCE SEEKING

What happens when you continue to seek reassurance from others, even after it has already been provided? In the following sections, we will examine the consequences to your relationships (interpersonal) and to you as an individual (intrapersonal).

Interpersonal Consequences

Because excessive reassurance seeking is repetitive and difficult to satisfy, significant others may become confused, frustrated, and irritated and thus increasingly likely to reject the reassurance seeker. Think back to Sylvia's responses to Eddie's requests for assurance. At first, she willingly gave him the assurance he desired. With repeated requests, however, she became increasingly frustrated by Eddie's unwillingness to accept her assurance. In the end, she became exasperated with Eddie and responded somewhat harshly to him.

Now, imagine that this type of interaction occurs again, and then again later, and keeps on occurring. Eventually, Sylvia may become so frustrated with Eddie that she shuts him out emotionally, is insensitive to his requests, or even ends their relationship. The result is that Eddie's fear of being rejected by Sylvia comes true. The rejection and disruption of his relationship leaves him socially isolated, and his depressive symptoms become worse as a result.

Several research studies have found that this pattern of excessive reassurance seeking and subsequent rejection occurs across different types of relationships, including married couples, dating couples, and college roommates (Benazon 2000; Joiner, Alfano, and Metalsky 1992, 1993; Katz and Beach 1997). These studies consistently indicate that people who are depressed are viewed negatively or rejected by others when they seek reassurance excessively. What's more, it doesn't appear to be the case that depression as such leads to rejection; rather, it appears that the combination of depression and excessive reassurance seeking has particularly damaging effects on relationships (Joiner and Metalsky 1995).

Intrapersonal Consequences

Clearly, excessive reassurance seeking can disrupt your relationships with others. But what happens to *you* when you repeatedly ask for assurances? Research studies consistently find that people who seek reassurance excessively are more likely to develop depression. It is important to note that not all people who become depressed excessively seek reassurance and not all people who seek reassurance become depressed. Obviously, there are many potential pathways of depression. Nevertheless, going overboard in seeking reassurance makes it much more likely that you will become more depressed. For example, consider Ashley's story.

■ Ashley

Ashley was a woman in her twenties with a lot going for her. She had recently completed medical school, was working her way through a residency program in pediatrics, and was engaged to be married. Unfortunately, she also happened to be in the midst of a major depressive episode. Her depression was relatively mild, in that she was still able to meet the demands of a hectic residency schedule and maintain a meaningful romantic relationship. However, her relationship had been deteriorating recently, and it was her relationship troubles that led her to seek treatment for depression.

Ashley reported a decline in the quality of her relationship with her fiancé, Mark, over the past year. They had been arguing and fighting more, there was less warmth than they had previously enjoyed, and there was a new a sense of tension in their relationship. Ashley questioned whether she should get married, and even though Mark had not directly said anything to indicate it, she suspected that he was also having second thoughts about their future together.

Ashley was fairly in tune with her thoughts and feelings, and she recognized that something was amiss soon after their relationship difficulties began. She initially thought things would work themselves out after they each grew accustomed to the changes in schedule and lifestyle associated with a medical residency. But as the arguments and frustrations continued and Ashley's depression became worse, she decided to visit her primary care physician.

Her doctor recognized that she was battling with depression, and he prescribed an antidepressant medication for her. After a few weeks of taking the medicine, Ashley's mood improved somewhat, and she saw a mild improvement in her sleeping and appetite. What's more, her fiancé seemed more patient and understanding, and their relationship improved for a little while. Nevertheless, some other depressive symptoms persisted even after Ashley had been taking medication for several months, and the relationship improvement was short-lived. At that point, Ashley came to us for help.

As we discussed what brought her in for treatment, several things became clear. First, Ashley's depression and her relationship problems were so closely related that it was virtually impossible to separate one from the other. That is, her mood both affected and was affected by her relationship. Second, Ashley cared deeply for her fiancé and sincerely desired to have a strong, lasting relationship with him. Third, certain things that Ashley said and did in her relationship with Mark set the stage for conflict, frustration, or disappointment. For example, she sometimes made unrealistic demands on Mark or held him to unrealistic standards, which usually resulted in her being disappointed in his failure to meet her standards. (Of course, certain things that Mark said and did also contributed to their relationship problems, but because Ashley sought treatment, we focused on what she could do to improve her depression rather than what he could do). Finally, conflict and disappointment in her relationship intensified her depression.

Often, when people experience relationship problems, many unresolved conflicts, strong emotions, and worries become jumbled together and seem overwhelming. Ashley was no exception to this, and making sense out of a complicated picture became an important task in treatment. To clarify the problem, Ashley selected specific instances of relationship problems that occurred between our sessions. Together, we analyzed exactly what Ashley said and did in these instances, trying to piece together common patterns of depressive symptoms and interpersonal conflict. We examined Ashley's actions in the context of what she wanted to get out of those situations and considered whether each behavior or thought helped her get what she desired out of her interactions with Mark.

Using this approach, we quickly identified that Ashley's excessive reassurance seeking led to relationship conflict with Mark, and it also led to a sense of rejection or distancing from him. As a result of her depression, Ashley often felt badly about herself and had difficulty making decisions. She strongly desired comfort and guidance from Mark—which he initially provided. Over time, however, he grew tired of her repeated requests for comfort and direction. He questioned why she wasn't able to figure things out on her own and why she continued to "nag" him with the same questions about whether he still loved her. His rejection added fuel to the fire of her insecurities, and she felt an even greater need for his assurances. Eventually, he shut the door emotionally, so to speak, and no longer provided affection and comfort. Ashley's fears of rejection had come true, and her depression spiraled downward.

Analysis

The key to Ashley's depression was in her relationships with others, especially her fiancé. Excessive reassurance seeking was a particularly important ingredient in their interpersonal strife, so we focused on stopping this behavior and replacing it with behaviors that led to healthier interactions. The process of monitoring and examining thoughts and actions in specific social interactions, then examining how they produced good or bad outcomes—an approach developed in part by McCullough (2000)—proved to be quite effective for Ashley. After recognizing how her excessive requests and demands had the unintended effect of actually pushing Mark away rather than bringing him closer, Ashley worked to address her fears of being unloved and to devote equal time to his needs and her needs.

THE PAINFUL PATH TO INTERPERSONAL REJECTION

A primary reason people seek reassurance excessively and rely too much upon others is that they fear being rejected, unloved, and the like. Ironically, and painfully, their fears often become reality through the very attempt to prevent them. That is, in an effort to ensure that they are not going to be abandoned, or that they are likeable, they actually make it more likely that others will reject them. This is certainly not intentional, and there is little use in speculating whether they are unconsciously motivated to sabotage relationships. However, there is practical benefit in recognizing that this pattern of social behavior leads to both depression and relationship problems.

If the material presented in this chapter rings true for you, then part of conquering your depression will require that you not rely on others too much. How do you do that? In the section that follows, we provide the answer.

CHALLENGE: BREAK THE HABIT OF REASSURANCE SEEKING

As was the case for Ashley, the challenge before you is to become self-assured rather than excessively seeking reassurances from others. To reach that goal, you'll follow a path similar to Ashley's. First, you'll monitor your reassurance seeking behaviors. Then, you'll examine and test the beliefs that underlie your tendencies to seek reassurance from others. Finally, you'll shift the focus of social interactions to others, so that their needs are receiving equal air time. We elaborate on each of these steps next.

EXERCISE 7.4: Breaking the Habit
of Reassurance Seeking

Step 1: Monitor Your Reassurance Seeking

Earlier in this chapter, we asked you to reflect upon when and under what circumstances you seek reassurance. Now, you must become a scientist and systematically observe when, where, and from whom you seek assurances. Select one or two specific interactions each day over the next week. For example, it could be a conversation over dinner with a romantic partner or a discussion on the phone with a friend or a family member. It is best to choose inter-actions with people who are very important to you, simply because it's more likely that you will seek reassurance from them and that your interactions with them will have a lasting impact on your depression.

After choosing a situation, use the Reassurance Seeking worksheet to briefly record what happened. In the "Situation" column, write down what you said and what the other person said. Next, in the "Relationship" column, list your conversation partner's relationship to you (for example, husband, sister, best friend). In the third column, rate the extent to which you sought reassurance from your conversation partner. Use a scale from 1 (did not seek reassurance) to 5 (sought much reassurance). Examples of seeking reassurance include asking others to confirm that you are doing things right, asking others if you are likeable or okay, asking if you are a good person, or asking if they love you or care about you. We have included a sample form to help you get started.

As you complete step 1 about subsequent situations, you may notice patterns in your tendencies to seek reassurance. For example, you may see that you tend to seek reassurance excessively in one particular relationship but not in others, or that you seek reassurance about one particular topic (for example, your work performance) more than others.

Step 2: Test Your Doubts

The next step in stopping excessive reassurance seeking, and thereby improving your depression, is to test the doubts that drive your reassurance seeking. That is, you must examine the accuracy of your thoughts and beliefs. In the "Underlying doubts" column, list your doubts or concerns that correspond to the situation described in the first column. For example, if you asked your wife several times whether she loves you, how much she cares about you, and so on, then your underlying doubt could be *My wife doesn't truly love me.*

Next, consider whether those doubts reflect reality or represent unrealistic fears. Is there a realistic basis for believing that your wife doesn't love you, or does this represent an unrealistic fear and a desire for comfort? Rate the degree to which each doubt is realistic on a scale from 1 (not realistic) to 5 (very realistic) in the final column on the form. As you complete multiple worksheets over time, you will likely see that many of the doubts that drive your reassurance seeking have little basis in reality and instead reflect unfounded fears.

Step 3: Shift the Focus

After you identify your patterns of excessive reassurance seeking and examine the doubts and fears that drive your requests for reassurance, the final step is to shift the focus of conversations to others. Seeking reassurance forces others to focus on you and your needs. That's perfectly natural some of the time, but it can lead to problems if it becomes excessive. Return to your Reassurance Seeking worksheets once more. Notice in which situations and with which conversation partners you most frequently ask for reassurance. The next time you interact with those people, try to focus on their experiences, needs, and feelings. You might do this by asking how their day was, following up on statements they make, or asking about their likes and interests. You may be surprised how much you find out. If you notice the conversation shifting to your needs—and if you realize that you're seeking assurances from others—try to redirect the conversation back to their interests. The goal here is not to completely shut yourself out of conversations but to give equal time and attention to both you and your companion.

Worksheet: Reassurance Seeking

Situation	Relationship	Did I seek reassurance? (1–5)	Underlying doubts	Realistic? (1–5)

Sample Reassurance Seeking Worksheet

Situation	Relationship	Did I seek reassurance? (1–5)	Underlying doubts	Realistic? (1–5)
Having dinner with my husband. I said, "You don't like the casserole I made, do you?" He said, "Yes, I like it." I asked him if he really liked it or was trying to be nice. He said he liked it. I asked if he thought it was too spicy. He said it wasn't and that it was fine. I said I was worried that it didn't turn out right. He told me not to worry, that it tasted fine.	Husband	5	My husband doesn't like my cooking and, by extension, doesn't like me.	1

8 Depression in the Home: Close Relations

Up to this point, we have discussed interpersonal behaviors that play a role in your depression in your relationships in general. These include your workplace or school relationships, your relationships with other acquaintances and friends, and your relationships with family members. In this chapter, we focus specifically on how your depression affects your closest, or most intimate, relationships: those with your immediate family members and with romantic partners such as boyfriends, girlfriends, or spouses.

DEPRESSION AND RELATIONSHIP SATISFACTION

As you may suspect, a substantial amount of research indicates that depression tends to damage close relationships. In particular, both you and your partner are more likely to be unsatisfied with the quality of your relationship when you are depressed (Burns, Sayers, and Moras 1994). This can range from general feelings of dissatisfaction with your relationship to more specific relationship problems such as difficulty communicating. Obviously, the specifics of any particular relationship dissatisfaction differ for every relationship. Exercise 8.1 will help stimulate thought about what areas of your close relationships might be most negatively affected by your depression.

EXERCISE 8.1:   How Does Depression Affect Your Close Relationships?

When you are depressed, do you tend to feel closer to, more distant from, or no different in your relationships with your significant other or immediate family members? If you feel more distant, in what ways? For example, *I withdraw and keep to myself more when I'm depressed* or *I feel like my family doesn't enjoy being around me when I'm depressed.*

_____

_____

_____

List specific examples of how your depression harms your close relationships. For example, *I feel like I don't have enough energy to devote attention to my wife's needs and wishes* or *I'm more irritable and snap at my boyfriend when I'm depressed.*

_____

_____

_____

In what ways do you think your depression affects your significant other or family members? For example, *My husband becomes grumpy when I feel blue* or *My parents seem sad when I feel down.*

_____

_____

_____

What do you notice from your responses to the questions in this exercise? Does it appear that depression tends to have a negative effect on the quality of your relationships and on those who are close to you? Research suggests that depression can impair close relationships in a number of ways. For example, people who are depressed report greater dissatisfaction in their close relationships, more feelings of anger toward their partners or spouses, and more frequent arguing with their partners and spouses (Fiske and Peterson 1991). In addition, they feel that their partners and close companions are more hostile toward them, hurt them more frequently, and provide less social support for them (Belsher and Costello 1991; Fiske and Peterson 1991; Thompson, Whiffen, and Blain 1995). As these examples clearly illustrate, you are likely to experience at least some distress and negativity in the context of your close relationships when you are depressed.

But what about your partner's perspective? That is, how do spouses or partners of depressed people view their relationships? Research suggests that spouses also experience anger and hostility in their interactions with their depressed partners (Goldman and Haaga 1995). What's more, the severity of depression goes hand in hand with the quality of the relationship: as depression gets worse, so does relationship quality (Judd et al. 2000). Sadly, in some cases it appears that depression may wipe out close relationships altogether (Mulder et al. 1996).

As you likely saw from completing exercise 8.1, your depression probably has a negative impact on your relationships. An important question therefore is, Which came first? That is, did you become depressed because you were having difficulties in your close relationships, or do you have difficulties in your close relationships because you are depressed?

Which Came First: The Chicken or the Egg?

Just as would-be philosophers (and perhaps farmers) have debated whether the chicken or the egg came first, psychologists have debated whether depression or relationship distress comes first. Before we discuss what research reveals about that debate, we encourage you to consider that question in your own life.

EXERCISE 8.2:   Which Came First: The Chicken or the Egg?

Think back to when your current episode of depression started.

If you were married or in a romantic relationship when your current episode of depression began, list stressors or points of conflict that were occurring in your relationship at that time. If you weren't in a romantic relationship at that time, answer the question with regard to your closest relationship (for example, best friend or brother).

_____

_____

_____

Did the stressors and conflicts you listed above occur before you became depressed?

_____

If not, would you say that your close relationships were running relatively smoothly until you became depressed, and then you started to notice more conflicts and problems?

_____

If your relationship problems did not begin until after you became depressed, list some examples of the types of problems that developed in your relationship after you became depressed.

_____

_____

_____

We imagine that those questions were difficult for you to answer, primarily because your relationships and your moods are so closely tied together. In fact, research suggests that the beginnings of depression and relationship strife are difficult to tease apart because depression and close relationship distress operate reciprocally (Davila 2001). That is, depression has a negative impact upon the quality of close relationships, and relationship distress has a negative impact upon your mood and worsens your depression. However, a very interesting pattern of findings has emerged with regard to gender. It appears as though, in general, women are more likely to experience increases in depression following problems in close relationships, but men are more likely to experience relationship distress subsequent to their depression (Fincham et al. 1997).

Regardless of which preceded the other in your particular case, it's clear that depression and close relationship distress, once established, tend to feed into one another. The bad news, of course, is that a setback in either of these two areas may lead to a setback in the other. The good news, however, is that by bringing about improvement in one area, you can bring about positive change in the other. This means that your depression can improve if you work to improve the quality of your close relationships. Before we turn to a discussion of how to do that, let's examine a final way in which your depression can affect your close relationships.

CONTAGIOUS DEPRESSION

In this scenario, when you're depressed, those around you may also begin to feel depressed. This is *contagious depression*. Can depression really be contagious? If I'm depressed, can you become depressed just by being near me? Well, not in the same sense that a virus is contagious. That is, depression isn't transmitted through physical contact or airborne particles. However, it does appear that your moods—including depressed mood—can rub off on those around you. Think for a moment about movies, television shows, or books. As you watch shows or read books, you experience temporary changes in your mood consistent with the emotional content of the program or book. For example, if we were to ask you to describe your mood while watching a movie such as *Schindler's List, The Silence of the Lambs,* or *Seven,* it would be quite unexpected for you to respond that you felt happy. In contrast, if we asked you to describe your mood while watching your favorite comedian perform, you would probably respond that you felt happy. Clearly, then, your moods are influenced by the emotional tone of your surroundings.

Now, let's apply that to your interpersonal surroundings, or your close relationships with other people. Do you notice temporary differences in your moods depending on whom you are around? Many people report that they feel somewhat happier and more energetic when they are around others who appear cheerful and enthusiastic. On the flip side, research suggests that being in the presence of angry, agitated, or otherwise disgruntled people can lead you to experience similar negative feelings (Schachter and Singer 1962). In that sense, not only are your moods influenced by your interpersonal surroundings, but you may even "catch" your moods from those around you, and they may "catch" your moods.

Of course, the point here is not to blame someone else for your negative moods or to blame yourself if others "catch" your depressed mood. Indeed, there is nothing active or intentional about contagious mood. Rather, it is simply something that you should be aware of and learn to master as you work to solve your depression. Before we discuss how contagious mood may be affecting you, let's first review what research has shown about contagious depression.

Research on Contagious Depression

After early research on general mood contagion, psychologists became increasingly interested in determining whether strongly negative and longer-lasting moods such as depression could be transmitted through interactions with other people. Many studies throughout the 1980s and 1990s investigated contagious depression in different ways, and the overwhelming conclusion is that depressed mood can indeed be transmitted through social interaction. That is, being around others who are depressed makes it more likely that you will experience both temporary depressed mood and persistent depressive symptoms such as major depression.

To make matters worse, depression not only tends to have a depressing effect upon others but also makes it more likely that others will reject you or not want to be around you. Here again, scientific evidence indicates that you are at a greater risk for being rejected or treated with hostility when you are depressed (Joiner and Katz 1999). Why might that be?

How Contagious Depression Works

The answer to that question is probably complex, but at least some evidence indicates that others' perceptions of depressed people contribute to both contagious depression and rejection of depressed people (Sacco 1999; Sacco and Dunn 1990). Researchers like Bill Sacco have found that your relationship partners develop mental representations of you that guide how they view you. This is a general pattern present in virtually all relationships, and the same is true for relationships in which one partner is depressed. However, when you are depressed, your relationship partner's mental representation of you tends to be qualitatively different. Allow us to explain.

Interestingly, when a depressed person experiences a negative event, people are likely to view it as the depressed person's own fault. For example, if you lose your job and you also happen to be depressed, people are more likely to blame you for losing your job. They might say it's because you weren't good at your job, you were lazy, or you were incompetent in some other regard. In contrast, people are more likely to think that the same negative event, when happening to someone who isn't depressed, is caused by external and uncontrollable factors such as major job layoffs or the closing of a plant. It doesn't seem fair, does it? Unfortunately, that's not the end of the story.

When depressed people experience a positive event such as a job promotion, others tend to view it as the result of luck or some other factor outside of the depressed person's control. Once again, when the same event occurs to someone who is not depressed, others believe that the nondepressed person played a role in obtaining the positive outcome. That is, they may say it's because you're smart, a good worker, and so on. The resulting picture, as we're sure you have noticed by now, is that depressed people are blamed more for negative events and given less credit for positive events.

Unfortunately, the story still doesn't end there. By carrying their research a step further, Sacco and Dunn (1990) found that people's perceptions (also called *attributions*) about the causes of negative events predicted how they responded emotionally to the person who experienced the negative event. That is, depressed people were viewed as being the cause of negative events in their lives, and that perception led others to feel angry toward them and unwilling to interact with them. In contrast, nondepressed people were viewed as experiencing negative events because of factors outside of their control, and as a result, people reported feeling concerned about them and willing to help them. Similar patterns regarding perceptions and emotional reactions are seen among spouses of depressed people (Sacco, Dumont, and Dow 1993). That is, if you are depressed, your spouse is more likely to blame you when bad things happen, to disregard your role in making good things happen, and to respond to you in an emotionally negative manner.

So others make negative judgments about you regardless of whether you experience good or bad outcomes, and these negative judgments then lead to feelings of hostility and rejection toward you. As if these attributions and emotional reactions to depressed people weren't enough, the story continues a step further. Once people develop these attributions, they remain the same, regardless of whether you remain depressed or get better. These attributions are, of course, initially influenced by your actual behavior, especially while you are in a depressive episode. However, once developed, they tend to take on an autonomous quality, in that they shape others' expectations of you and lead them to focus on those things that confirm their image of you.

This explains why others may reject you when you're depressed (and perhaps even as you start to get better), but it still doesn't explain how depression can be contagious. Our research suggests that excessive reassurance seeking, as we described in chapter 7, likely plays a key role in the contagious nature of depression (Katz, Beach, and Joiner 1999; Joiner 1994). In general, we have found that when people are both depressed and engaging in a lot of reassurance seeking, their partners are more likely to develop depressive symptoms themselves. Taken together with the process by which depression leads to interpersonal rejection, as we just described, the research on contagious depression suggests that the combination of depression and excessive reassurance seeking distances your significant others from you. This happens in both a literal sense, in that they may become hostile or rejecting, and in an emotional sense, in that they may become depressed and emotionally unavailable.

Now, take a moment to reflect back to chapter 7, in which we discussed excessive reassurance seeking. Based upon the results of exercise 7.3, do you tend to seek reassurances from others, perhaps excessively? If so, then you may be more likely to receive rejecting responses from others. Furthermore, the likelihood of contagious depression, in which others feel depressed when they are around you, also becomes greater. We say that not with the goal of making you feel guilty, because there is nothing intentional about the process of contagious depression. It simply is what it is, and it is important for you to know about it so you can stop the cycle and improve your relationships with other people.

Of course, we hope that you are now actively monitoring your reassurance seeking, testing the doubts that drive your requests for assurances, and working to shift the focus of conversations to others' experiences and feelings. If you haven't started doing that, then we strongly encourage you to do so now. By carrying out the challenge at the end of chapter 7, you will likely reduce the harm depression causes in your relationships, including rejection by others.

◼ Ray

Ray was certainly not the typical case of depression. Most people first experience depression during late adolescence or in their twenties or thirties. Ray had recently celebrated his sixty-eighth birthday—and was also in the middle of his first depressive episode. And while the onset of Ray's depression was much later than the norm, there was little doubt that he was depressed. He had the telltale symptoms: persistent feelings of sadness, lethargy, loss of interest in life, difficulty sleeping at night followed by frequent dozing off during the day, and feelings of guilt about being depressed. Fortunately, Ray was not entertaining thoughts of suicide, although he did passively wish that he "would just hurry up and die."

The fact that Ray was in his late sixties and just now experiencing his first depressive episode raised the question of what triggered, or set into motion, his depression. As we chatted, Ray described a gradual descent into depression following his retirement just over one year ago. He said that although he had always looked forward to retirement, the transition from working life to retired life had not been easy. Much of his identity and social connections were tied to work, and suddenly "losing all that" after forty years had left a big hole in his life.

The constant in his life had been Shirley, his wife of forty-five years. Ray said that he and Shirley had been together long enough to know just about everything about each other: "the good, the bad, and the ugly," in his words. Like his mood, however, their relationship had deteriorated over the past year. They argued more, had more conflicts, and experienced a tension that hadn't previously existed in their marriage. At first, Ray attributed this conflict to the increased amount of time they spent together following his retirement and to the process of readjusting to new roles. But rather than improving with time, the quality of their relationship continued to sink.

Because their relationship was so important to both of them and so dramatically affected by Ray's depression, we decided that it would be helpful for Shirley to attend some therapy sessions with Ray. As we talked, it became clear that Shirley had also begun to experience depressive symptoms over the past several months. Her symptoms weren't severe enough to warrant a diagnosis of major depression, but they were still distressing to Shirley.

Shirley's description of their relationship quality mirrored her husband's: increased arguing, hostility, and tension, along with less happiness and fewer displays of affection. Shirley also described how Ray had grown increasingly "needy" or dependent upon her. He repeatedly asked her to verify that he was okay and that he was doing things correctly (paying the correct bills, for example), and he even asked her to make routine decisions for him, such as what he would eat or what clothes he would wear. In the course of their forty-five-year marriage, Shirley had become accustomed to Ray being independent and decisive, and she had difficulty understanding and adjusting to her husband's seemingly juvenile behavior. To be frank, she didn't like it and thought it was time for him to "start acting like the man she married."

Analysis

Ray was a physically healthy man in his late sixties who had not previously been depressed, so by all accounts, he would be considered at low risk for developing depression. However, a change in the structure of Ray's life led to a change in his activities and social connections, and he subsequently spiraled into a depressive episode. What's more, the quality of his long-term relationship with his wife was also pulled down into the mire of depression, and she likewise began to experience depressive symptoms.

Although Ray developed depression later in life than is typical, the pattern of depression and worsening relationship functioning tends to be the rule rather than the exception. What is perhaps most remarkable is that a stable, happy partnership of over forty years was dramatically damaged by depression. In fact, Shirley's own views of her husband changed from independent and decisive to dependent and needy over the course of just a few months. What went wrong?

As Ray became more depressed, their relationship included more hostile, negative exchanges and fewer positive interactions. This was probably due to a number of factors, including Ray's persistent negative, gloomy mood and Shirley's frustration with his inability to adapt to life after work. In particular, notice Shirley's description of Ray as needy and dependent. As his depression worsened, Ray began to ask Shirley for more and more assurances and feedback about his own worth and about minor details. As we discussed earlier in this chapter, the combination of depression and excessive reassurance seeking holds negative consequences for all parties involved. For the depressed person, it brings about rejection, and clearly it did bring hostile reactions from Shirley. For the partner of the depressed person, it can bring about contagious depressive symptoms, as Shirley experienced.

Notice also how Ray's and Shirley's experiences were consistent with the research finding that men often experience close relationship distress following the onset of depression, while women often experience depression following the onset of close relationship distress (Fincham et al. 1997). Ray's depressive experiences strained his relationship with Shirley and reduced their relationship quality, and once their relationship began to decline, Shirley started to experience depressive symptoms of her own.

FROM PARENT TO CHILD: THE "GIFT" OF DEPRESSION

Not only are marital and romantic relationships intertwined with and harmed by depression, but other types of close relationships are also damaged by depression. In particular, the relations between parents and children are primary channels through which depression can be communicated. If you are a parent, your depression may affect your child in numerous ways. For example, depression can hinder your ability to effectively parent your child. Depressed parents, similar to depressed spouses, tend to be more negative and critical and less positive and cohesive in their interactions with their children (Jacob and Johnson 2001; Kaslow et al. 1992).

Unfortunately, children of depressed parents are at six times the risk for developing depression themselves and often do so at a young age (Gotlib and Goodman 1999). While this is probably due to a variety of causes, including genetic and biological factors, research indicates that social interactions with depressed parents can contribute to the occurrence of depression among youngsters (Brennan et al. 2002). Once again, this is not meant to make you feel guilty if you are a depressed parent. Rather, understanding the processes at work is a crucial step in putting an end to the cycle of depression.

CHALLENGE: IMPROVE YOUR RELATIONSHIPS BY CHANGING YOUR INTERACTIONS

As you have seen in this chapter, depression likely hurts the quality of your close personal relationships, including those with your spouse or romantic partner and your children. Your relations may become more negative and critical, and you may sense rejection and hostility even in the context of these close relationships. Finally, your depression may be contagious in that others may develop depressive symptoms over time from interacting with you. Of course, it could be that your depression developed because someone close to you was depressed. Either way, depression is present in the relationship and is likely keeping your relationship from being as healthy as it could be.

What to do? Well, there is no simple answer to that question, but the good news is that you already have the tools available to improve your close relationships. By learning the principles and techniques that we discussed in chapters 2 through 7 and applying them specifically in the context of your close relationships, you will see marked improvement in the quality of these relationships. Given the connection between relationship quality and depression, we expect that you will feel less depressed as your close relations improve. That is, by altering the way you interact with your spouse, partner, children, or whomever you are closest to, you can expect to improve the quality of your relationships and improve your depression.

Rather than trying to apply all six challenge techniques simultaneously, which could be overwhelming, we encourage you to focus on one or two that seem most relevant to your relationship. In the case of Ray and Shirley, for example, focusing on Ray's excessive reassurance seeking would have been a fruitful approach. For others, focusing on negative feedback seeking (chapter 6) or self-handicapping (chapter 5) may be more beneficial. Don't become preoccupied with choosing the absolute best challenge technique for your close relationship. For one thing, we anticipate that using any of the techniques will be helpful to a certain extent. Furthermore, we encourage you to focus on other challenges after you have successfully applied the first one you select. In that way, you can eventually work your way through each of the six challenges in your close relationships.

We also want to remind you that relationship changes may not happen immediately. Remember that the people close to you have grown accustomed to the way you act around them, even if some of your actions are not healthy for the relationship. They may be somewhat unsure how to react when they see you doing things differently. That's okay—that's just a part of the process in improving your relationships. Hang in there and keep practicing the techniques in this book, and those around you will begin to respond favorably to your efforts.

9   Tying It All Together

In chapters 2 through 7, we presented six interpersonal processes integral to depression and discussed how each process contributes to your depression. We discussed the processes separately for conceptual reasons (these are distinguishable processes), for presentational reasons (it is easier to present and understand one process at a time), and for treatment reasons (it is easier to target one type of behavior for change at a time). Despite our distinction between these six processes, we emphasize that they are not entirely independent. If you are depressed, then you probably experience difficulties in most, if not all, of the processes we have described. In this chapter, we discuss how these processes overlap and how change in one area may naturally lead to change in another area. We also use this chapter to review and integrate the challenges from chapters 2 through 7 and caution you about potential setbacks and possible resistance from others.

REVIEWING AND INTEGRATING THE SIX PROCESSES

We began this book by describing depression, its symptoms and typical courses, and its interpersonal nature. At this point, we encourage you to revisit and complete exercise 1.1, "Assessing the Symptoms of Your Depression," then compare your current depressive symptoms with those when you began this book. We hope that you are less depressed now than you were the first time you completed that exercise. If your symptoms haven't changed much, then we suggest that you continue to rigorously apply the principles in this book to your relationships. It may take time before you see improvements, but be assured that your relationships (and your depression) will improve.

In chapter 2, we described the nature of interpersonal behaviors among depressed people in general and encouraged you to examine your social behaviors in detail. In particular, we distinguished between the "how" and the "what" of depressive communication. The challenge for chapter 2 was to monitor and record both the content (the "what") and the process (the "how") of your interactions with other people. To boost the improvements you have made, you may wish to reevaluate how you're doing in terms of content and process. Are you making good eye contact when you speak with others? Do you tend to talk about negative topics? Unless you continue to actively work on these things until they become habitual, it can be easy to slide back into old routines, particularly with regard to the nonverbal behaviors that go along with depression (such as frowning, speaking softly, and avoiding eye contact).

In chapter 3, we discussed research on the social skills of depressed people and talked about differing perceptions of social skills. We challenged you to develop an accurate view of your own social skills by conducting social experiments in which you monitored your performance in social situations and tested some of your beliefs about your social skills.

In chapter 4, we explored the damaging effects of interpersonal inhibition and discussed how it promotes depression. In particular, we highlighted the avoidance of interpersonal conflict as a key to depression, and we described how overcoming fears about interpersonal conflict could improve your relationships and reduce your depression. We challenged you to do so by examining your behaviors in social interactions and identifying ways that you could act more assertively.

In chapter 5, we covered self-handicapping, or selling yourself short, and discussed how it can lead to chronic underachievement. We discussed the role of self-handicapping in depression as well as the importance of self-esteem in self-handicapping. We ended chapter 5 with a challenge to go out on a limb, confront feared performance situations, and open yourself to the possibility of not performing as well as you would like.

Chapter 6 emphasized negative feedback seeking, or asking for the worst. We explained why depressed people often seek negative appraisals from others and the untoward consequences of receiving negative feedback. We challenged you to change the mental filter that leads you to ask for the worst, to do things that you enjoy as a way of temporarily improving self-esteem, and to then specifically seek (and accept) feedback about your positive qualities.

Finally, we discussed interpersonal dependence in chapter 7, highlighting the importance of excessive reassurance seeking to depression. We challenged you to become self-assured by monitoring your reassurance seeking, testing hypotheses about your doubts, and shifting the focus of conversations to others' interests rather than maintaining the focus on yourself.

When you combine these six chapters and practice their corresponding exercises, you will develop a social interaction style that includes assertive speech, nonverbal behaviors that convey self-confidence and interest in others, a willingness to accept positive comments about yourself, and the ability to make decisions and function independently. These characteristics don't imply arrogance, aggression, or haughtiness. Rather, they suggest that you feel good about yourself and that you value your interactions with others. When those around you see these behaviors, they will likely respond with appropriate respect and appreciation, and they will value their relationships with you.

Contrast that picture with the view that people who are depressed have poor relationships characterized by negativity, hostility, and rejection, and we think you'll agree that the exercises in this book are well worth the effort.

HOW THE PROCESSES MAY BE INTERRELATED

There are times when two or more of the processes described in chapters 2 through 7 may overlap. Many combinations are possible, and we obviously can't discuss them all in this book. However, we would like to point out a few of the most likely combinations and emphasize how changing one of the processes may affect another behavior.

A single statement may accomplish more than one result. For example, making the statement, "I'm just no good as a spouse" may invite confirmation that you are a bad spouse (an example of negative feedback seeking), may reduce others' expectations of your future performance as a spouse (an example of self-handicapping), or may request reassurance that you are actually a good spouse (an example of excessive reassurance seeking). Because negative feedback seeking, self-handicapping, and excessive reassurance seeking may all overlap this way, your efforts to change any one of these processes can lead to changes in the other two, at least in some instances.

There are other situations in which the processes can compound one another. That is, the effects of one process may intensify the negative effects of another process. For example, the impact of excessive reassurance seeking and negative feedback seeking on your relationships may be compounded by interpersonal avoidance. If you avoid interacting with others, you likely have few relationships on which to rely, and the consequences of excessive reassurance seeking and negative feedback seeking may be concentrated on just one or two relationships. Hence, just as a lens may intensely focus sunlight on one spot, avoidance may focus excessive reassurance seeking and negative feedback seeking on one relationship. In this sense, interpersonal avoidance may intensify the harm of excessive reassurance seeking and negative feedback seeking. The flip side is that as you become more assertive in your close relationships, the negative consequences of asking for the worst and excessive reassurance seeking may diminish.

As a final example of interrelations between the processes, consider how avoiding interpersonal conflict may encourage self-handicapping regarding social and interpersonal performance. That is, in an effort to avoid conflict with others, you may sell yourself short. The statement, "I'm just no good at handling conflict" may allow you to avoid conflict with others and simultaneously reduce their expectations of you. Here again, developing and implementing stronger assertiveness skills may reduce your desire to sell yourself short.

SOME FINAL WORDS OF ENCOURAGEMENT

As we conclude this book, we want to extend some words of encouragement and preparation. Depression can be difficult, draining, and demoralizing. We realize that there may be times when the hopelessness and despair that go along with depression may discourage you from actively carrying out the exercises in this book. Nevertheless, we encourage you to steadfastly apply these principles in your life, even when it is difficult to do so.

Consider the analogy of a marathon runner. Once a person has made the decision to run, she does not immediately go out and run a full twenty-six-mile marathon. (She most certainly wouldn't get very far.) Rather, she begins running short distances, such as a mile or even half of a mile. Gradually, and with physical exertion and some degree of pain, she increases the distance she can run. With time, effort, and repeated practice, she is eventually able to complete a full twenty-six-mile marathon.

Similarly, your battle with depression is more a marathon than a short sprint. With continued practice, effort, and at times even discomfort, utilizing the techniques described in this book will lead to improvements in your interpersonal relationships and in your depression.

Along those same lines, we want to remind you that you may initially experience negative reactions from those around you as you begin to change your social behaviors. The reason for this is not that they want you to be depressed. Rather, they have grown accustomed to the way you usually act. If you are typically unassertive and agree to even outlandish requests from others, they may become frustrated or angry when you stand up for yourself. Over time, however, they will adapt to the new limits that you set, and they will begin to respect your assertiveness. The point is simply to stay the course, even when there are bumps in the road. In the long run, you will reap the dividends of your persistent efforts: better relationships and better moods.

References

Alloy, L. B., and L. Y. Abramson. 1982. Learned helplessness, depression, and the illusion of control. *Journal of Personality and Social Psychology* 42 (6): 1114–26.

American Psychiatric Association. 1994. *Diagnostic and Statistical Manual of Mental Disorders* 4th ed. Washington, D.C.: American Psychiatric Association.

Amore, M., and M. C. Jori. 2001. Faster response on amisulpride 50 mg versus sertraline 50–100 mg in patients with dysthymia or double depression: A randomized, double-blind, parallel group study. *International Clinical Psychopharmacology* 16 (6): 317–24.

Ball, S. G., M. W. Otto, M. H. Pollack, and J. F. Rosenbaum. 1994. Predicting prospective episodes of depression in patients with panic disorder: A longitudinal study. *Journal of Consulting and Clinical Psychology* 62:359–65.

Baumgardner, A. H. 1991. Claiming depressive symptoms as a self-handicap: A protective self-presentation strategy. *Basic and Applied Social Psychology* 12 (1): 97–113.

Beck, A. T. 1976. *Cognitive Therapy and the Emotional Disorders.* New York: International Universities Press.

Belsher, G., and C. G. Costello. 1991. Do confidants of depressed women provide less social support than confidants of nondepressed women? *Journal of Abnormal Psychology* 100:516–25.

Benazon, N. R. 2000. Predicting negative spousal attributions toward depressed persons: A test of Coyne's interpersonal model. *Journal of Abnormal Psychology* 109:550–54.

Brennan, P. A., C. Hammen, A. R. Katz, and R. M. Le Brocque. 2002. Maternal depression, paternal psychopathology, and adolescent diagnostic outcomes. *Journal of Consulting and Clinical Psychology* 70:1075–85.

Buchwald, A. M., and D. Rudick-Davis. 1993. The symptoms of major depression. *Journal of Abnormal Psychology* 102 (2): 197–205.

Burns, D. D., S. L. Sayers, and K. Moras. 1994. Intimate relationships and depression: Is there a causal connection? *Journal of Consulting and Clinical Psychology* 62 (5): 1033–43.

Cheek, J. M., and A. H. Buss. 1981. Shyness and sociability. *Journal of Personality and Social Psychology* 41:330–39.

Coyne, J. C. 1976. Toward an interactional description of depression. *Psychiatry* 39:28–40

Davila, J. 2001. Paths to unhappiness: The overlapping courses of depression and romantic dysfunction. In *Marital and Family Processes in Depression: A Scientific Foundation for Clinical Practice*, edited by S. R. H. Beach. Washington, D.C.: American Psychological Association.

Fincham, F. D., S. R. H. Beach, G. T. Harold, and L. N. Osborne. 1997. Marital satisfaction and depression: Different causal relationships for men and women? *Psychological Science* 8:351–57.

Fiske, V., and C. Peterson. 1991. Love and depression: The nature of depressive romantic relationships. *Journal of Social and Clinical Psychology* 10:75–90.

Ganchrow, J. R., J. E. Steiner, M. Kleiner, and E. L. Edelstein. 1978. A multidisciplinary approach to the expression of pain in psychotic depression. *Perceptual and Motor Skills* 47:379–90.

Giesler, R. B., R. A. Josephs, and W. B. Swann. 1996. Self-verification in clinical depression: The desire for negative evaluation. *Journal of Abnormal Psychology* 105:358–68.

Goldman, L., and D. A. F. Haaga. 1995. Depression and the experience and expression of anger in marital and other relationships. *Journal of Nervous and Mental Disease* 183:505–9.

Gotlib, I. H., and S. H. Goodman. 1999. Children of parents with depression. In *Developmental Issues in the Clinical Treatment of Children*, edited by W. K. Silverman and T. H. Ollendick. Needham Heights, Mass.: Allyn and Bacon.

Hammen, C. 1999. The emergence of an interpersonal approach to depression. In *The Interactional Nature of Depression*, edited by T. E. Joiner, Jr. and J. C. Coyne. Washington, D.C.: American Psychological Association.

Jacob, T., and S. L. Johnson. 2001. Sequential interactions in the parent-child communications of depressed fathers and depressed mothers. *Journal of Family Psychology* 15:38–52.

Joiner, T. E., Jr. 1994. Contagious depression: Existence, specificity to depressed symptoms, and the role of reassurance seeking. *Journal of Personality and Social Psychology* 67:287–96.

———. 1995. The price of soliciting and receiving negative feedback: Self-verification theory as a vulnerability to depression theory. *Journal of Abnormal Psychology* 104:364–72.

———. 1997. Shyness and low social support as interactive diatheses, and loneliness as mediator: Testing an interpersonal-personality view of depression. *Journal of Abnormal Psychology* 106:386–94.

Joiner, T. E., Jr., M. S. Alfano, and G. I. Metalsky. 1992. When depression breeds contempt: Reassurance-seeking, self-esteem, and rejection of depressed college students by their roommates. *Journal of Abnormal Psychology* 101:165–73.

Joiner, T. E., Jr., M. S. Alfano, and G. I. Metalsky. 1993. Caught in the crossfire: Depression, self-consistency, self-enhancement, and the response of others. *Journal of Social and Clinical Psychology* 12:113–34.

Joiner, T. E., Jr., and J. Katz. 1999. Contagion of depressive symptoms and mood: Meta-analytic review and explanations from cognitive, behavioral, and interpersonal viewpoints. *Clinical Psychology and Science Practice* 6:149–64.

Joiner, T. E., Jr., and J. Kistner. 2004. On seeing clearly and thriving: Interpersonal perspicacity as adaptive (not depressive) realism (or where three theories meet). Manuscript under review.

Joiner, T. E., Jr., and G. I. Metalsky. 1995. A prospective test of an integrative interpersonal theory of depression: A naturalistic study of college roommates. *Journal of Social and Clinical Psychology* 69:778–88.

Jones, E. E., and S. Berglas. 1978. Control of attributions about the self through self-handicapping strategies: The appeal of alcohol and the role of underachievement. *Personality and Social Psychology Bulletin* 4 (2): 200–206.

Judd, L. L., H. S. Akiskal, and M. P. Paulus. 1997. The role and clinical significance of subsyndromal depressive symptoms (SSD) in unipolar major depressive disorder. *Journal of Affective Disorders* 45 (1): 5–17.

Judd, L. J., H. S. Akiskal, P. J. Zeller, M. Paulus, A. C. Leon, J. D. Maser, J. Endicott, W. Coryell, J. L. Kunovac, T. I. Mueller, J. P. Rice, and M. B. Keller. 2000. Psychosocial disability during the long-term course of unipolar major depressive disorder. *Archives of General Psychiatry* 57:375–80.

Kaslow, N., V. Warner, K. John, and R. Brown. 1992. Intrainformant agreement and family functioning in depressed and nondepressed parents and their children. *American Journal of Family Therapy* 20:204–17.

Katz, J., and S. R. H. Beach. 1997. Romance in the crossfire: When do women's depressive symptoms predict partner relationship dissatisfaction? *Journal of Social and Clinical Psychology* 16:243–58.

Katz, J., S. R. H. Beach, and T. E. Joiner, Jr. 1999. Contagious depression in dating couples. *Journal of Social and Clinical Psychology* 18:1–13.

Kovacs, M., C. Gastonis, S. T. Paulauskas, and C. Richards. 1989. Depressive disorders in childhood: IV. A longitudinal study of comorbidity with and risk for anxiety disorders. *Archives of General Psychiatry* 46:776–82.

Lange, A., and P. Jakubowski. 1976. *Responsible Assertive Behavior*. Champaign, Ill.: Research Press.

Lara, M. E., J. Leader, and D. N. Klein. 1997. The association between social support and course of depression: Is it confounded with personality? *Journal of Abnormal Psychology* 106:478–82.

Leary, M. R., and J. A. Shepperd. 1986. Behavioral self-handicaps versus reported self-handicaps: A conceptual note. *Journal of Personality and Social Psychology* 51 (6): 1265–68.

Lewinsohn, P. M., and J. Libet. 1972. Pleasant events, activity schedules, and depressions. *Journal of Abnormal Psychology* 79:291–95.

Lewinsohn, P. M., W. Mischel, W. Chaplin, and R. Barton. 1980. Social competence and depression: The role of illusory self-perceptions. *Journal of Abnormal Psychology* 89:203–12.

Lewinsohn, P. M., A. Solomon, J. R. Seeley, and A. Zeiss. 2000. Clinical implications of "subthreshold" depressive symptoms. *Journal of Abnormal Psychology* 109 (2): 345–51.

McCullough, J. P., Jr. 2000. *Treatment for Chronic Depression: Cognitive Behavioral Analysis System of Psychotherapy (CBASP)*. New York: Guilford.

McLeod, J. D., R. C. Kessler, and K. R. Landis. 1992. Speed of recovery from major depressive episodes in a community sample of married men and women. *Journal of Abnormal Psychology* 101 (2): 277–86.

Mulder, R. T., P. R. Joyce, P. F. Sullivan, and M. A. Oakley-Browne. 1996. Intimate bonds in depression. *Journal of Affective Disorders* 40:175–78.

Pettit, J. W., and T. E. Joiner, Jr. 2001a. Negative feedback leads to an increase in depressed symptoms: Further support for self-verification theory as a vulnerability to depression theory. *Journal of Psychopathology and Behavioral Assessment* 23 (1): 69–74.

Pettit, J. W., and T. E. Joiner, Jr. 2001b. Negative life events predict negative feedback seeking as a function of impact on self-esteem. *Cognitive Therapy and Research* 25 (6): 733–41.

Rehm, L. P. 1977. A self-control model of depression. *Behavior Therapy* 8:787–804.

Rhodewalt, F., D. M. Sanbonmatsu, B. Tschanz, D. L. Feick, and A. Waller. 1995. Self-handicapping and interpersonal trade-offs: The effects of claimed self-handicaps on observers' performance evaluations and feedback. *Personality and Social Psychology Bulletin* 21 (10): 1042–50.

Rosenfarb, I. S., and J. Aron. 1992. The self-protective function of depressive affect and cognition. *Journal of Social and Clinical Psychology* 11 (4): 323–35.

Sacco, W. P. 1999. A social-cognitive model of interpersonal processes in depression. In *The Interactional Nature of Depression*, edited by T. E. Joiner, Jr. and J. C. Coyne. Washington, D.C.: American Psychological Association.

Sacco, W. P., C. P. Dumont, and M. G. Dow. 1993. Attributional, perceptual, and affective responses to depressed and nondepressed marital partners. *Journal of Consulting and Clinical Psychology* 61:1076–82.

Sacco, W. P., and V. K. Dunn. 1990. Effect of actor depression on observer attributions: Existence and impact of negative attributions toward the depressed. *Journal of Personality and Social Psychology* 59:517–24.

Schachter, S., and J. E. Singer. 1962. Cognitive, social, and physiological determinants of emotional state. *Psychological Review* 69:379–99.

Segrin, C. 1990. A meta-analytic review of social skill deficits in depression. *Communication Monographs* 57:292–308.

Segrin, C. 2000. *Interpersonal Processes in Psychological Problems*. New York: Guilford Press.

Segrin, C., and M. A. Fitzpatrick. 1992. Depression and verbal aggressiveness in different marital couple types. *Communication Studies* 43:79–91.

Seligman, M. E. P. 1998. Research in clinical psychology: Why is there so much depression today? In *The G. Stanley Hall Lecture Series*, edited by I. Cohen. Washington, D.C.: American Psychological Association.

Shakespeare, W. 1998. *Hamlet*. Philadelphia, Pa.: The University of Pennsylvania Press.

Sullivan, P. F., M. C . Neale, and K. S. Kendler. 2000. Genetic epidemiology of major depression: Review and meta-analysis. *American Journal of Psychiatry* 157: 1552–62.

Swann, W. B., Jr. 1990. To be known or to be adored: The interplay of self-enhancement and self-verification. In *Handbook of Motivation and Cognition, vol. 2*, edited by E. T. Higgins and R. M. Sorrentino. New York: Guilford.

Swann, W. B., Jr., R. M. Wenzlaff, D. S. Krull, and B. W. Pelham. 1992. Allure of negative feedback: Self-verification strivings among depressed persons. *Journal of Abnormal Psychology* 101:293–305.

Swann, W. B., Jr., R. M. Wenzlaff, and R. W. Tafarodi. 1992. Depression and the search for negative evaluations: More evidence of the role of self-verification strivings. *Journal of Abnormal Psychology* 101:314–17.

Thompson, J. M., V. E. Whiffen, and M. D. Blain. 1995. Depressive symptoms, sex, and perceptions of intimate relationships. *Journal of Social and Personal Relationships* 12:49–66.

Tice, D., and R. F. Baumeister. 1997. Longitudinal study of procrastination, performance, stress, and health: The costs and benefits of dawdling. *Psychological Science* 8:454–58.

Twain, M. 1999. *Wit and Wisdom of Mark Twain: A Book of Quotations.* New York: Dover Publications.

Youngren, M. A., and P. M. Lewinsohn. 1980. The functional relation between depression and problematic interpersonal behavior. *Journal of Abnormal Psychology* 89:333–41.

Zimbardo, P. G. 1977. *Shyness: What It Is, What to Do about It.* Reading, Mass.: Addison-Wesley.

Jeremy W. Pettit, Ph.D., is assistant professor of psychology at the University of Houston in Houston, TX. He completed his doctoral training at Florida State University in Tallahassee, FL. His primary area of interest centers on etiological and maintaining factors in depression spectrum disorders. His secondary interests include treatment of depression and biopsychosocial approaches to understanding and preventing suicide. He has published over thirty-five scientific journal articles and edited book chapters on these topics.

Thomas Ellis Joiner, Jr., Ph.D., attended Princeton University in Princeton, NJ, and received his Ph.D. in clinical psychology in 1993 from the University of Texas at Austin. He is Bright-Burton Professor of Psychology and director of the University Psychology Clinic at Florida State University in Tallahassee, FL. His recent papers on the psychology, neurobiology, and treatment of depression, suicidal behavior, anxiety, and eating disorders have received international attention. He is regarded as the current leading expert in interpersonal approaches to depression. Author of over 185 peer-reviewed publications and over 100 conference presentations, he has served as associate editor of **The Journal of Behavior Therapy** and sits on ten editorial boards, including those of the **Journal of Consulting and Clinical Psychology,** the **Journal of Abnormal Psychology,** and **Clinical Psychology: Science and Practice.**

Foreword writer **Lynn P. Rehm, Ph.D., ABPP,** is professor of psychology at the University of Houston in Houston, TX, and president-elect of the Division of Clinical and Community Psychology of the International Association of Applied Psychology.

Some Other
New Harbinger Titles

Angry All the Time, Item 3929 $13.95

Handbook of Clinical Psychopharmacology for Therapists, 4th edition, Item 3996 $55.95

Writing For Emotional Balance, Item 3821 $14.95

Surviving Your Borderline Parent, Item 3287 $14.95

When Anger Hurts, 2nd edition, Item 3449 $16.95

Calming Your Anxious Mind, Item 3384 $12.95

Ending the Depression Cycle, Item 3333 $17.95

Your Surviving Spirit, Item 3570 $18.95

Coping with Anxiety, Item 3201 $10.95

The Agoraphobia Workbook, Item 3236 $19.95

Loving the Self-Absorbed, Item 3546 $14.95

Transforming Anger, Item 352X $10.95

Don't Let Your Emotions Run Your Life, Item 3090 $17.95

Why Can't I Ever Be Good Enough, Item 3147 $13.95

Your Depression Map, Item 3007 $19.95

Successful Problem Solving, Item 3023 $17.95

Working with the Self-Absorbed, Item 2922 $14.95

The Procrastination Workbook, Item 2957 $17.95

Coping with Uncertainty, Item 2965 $11.95

The BDD Workbook, Item 2930 $18.95

You, Your Relationship, and Your ADD, Item 299X $17.95

The Stop Walking on Eggshells Workbook, Item 2760 $18.95

Conquer Your Critical Inner Voice, Item 2876 $15.95

The PTSD Workbook, Item 2825 $17.95

Hypnotize Yourself Out of Pain Now!, Item 2809 $14.95

The Depression Workbook, 2nd edition, Item 268X $19.95

Beating the Senior Blues, Item 2728 $17.95

Shared Confinement, Item 2663 $15.95

Getting Your Life Back Together When You Have Schizophrenia, Item 2736 $14.95

Do-It-Yourself Eye Movement Technique for Emotional Healing, Item 2566 $13.95

Call **toll free, 1-800-748-6273,** or log on to our online bookstore at **www.newharbinger.com** to order. Have your Visa or Mastercard number ready. Or send a check for the titles you want to New Harbinger Publications, Inc., 5674 Shattuck Ave., Oakland, CA 94609. Include $4.50 for the first book and 75¢ for each additional book, to cover shipping and handling. (California residents please include appropriate sales tax.) Allow two to five weeks for delivery.

Prices subject to change without notice.